The Literate Mode of Cicero's Legal Rhetoric

Richard Leo Enos

Southern Illinois University Press

Carbondale and Edwardsville

Printed in the United States of America
Edited by Sally Master
Designed by Heidi M. Gunter
Production supervised by Natalia Nadraga

91 90 89 88 4 3 2 1

Library of Congress Cataloging-in-Publication Data

Enos, Richard Leo.
The literate mode of Cicero's legal rhetoric.

Bibliography: p.
Includes index.
1. Forensic orations. 2. Roman law—Language. 3. Rhetoric.
4. Cicero, Marcus Tullius. I. Title.
KJA190.E56 1988 350.4'4 87-12670
ISBN 0-8093-1382-0

The paper used in this publication meets the minimum requirements of American National Standard for Information Sciences—Permanence of Paper for Printed Materials, ANSI Z39.48-1984. ∞™

To my wife, Jane Helppie,

and our children,

David, Alisa, James, Nathan, and Alexander

Contents

Preface

Quintilian has given us an excellent rule, in the very case: that we should be modest and circumspect, in passing a judgment on men so illustrious, lest, as it happens to the generality of censurers, we be found at last to condemn what we do not understand.

Conyers Middleton, The Life of M. Tullius Cicero

The scourge of Catiline. The archenemy of Mark Anthony. The champion of the Republic. These epithets characterize the Cicero who has delighted and even inspired readers for centuries. Cicero's numerous works have provided the gist that has moved readers and reconstructed the backbone of many Victorian politicians who, inspired by their boyhood reading of his achievements, spoke out in Parliament and court as (they believed) their Roman model would have. We have had centuries to scrutinize Cicero's works, to weigh and sift the evidence that will tell us more about this complex, fascinating individual. Yet, after all that examination is concluded, after all the historical accounts and meticulous biographies have been shelved for posterity, can we say that "our Cicero" is the most accurate portrait? The life of Marcus Tullius Cicero, and the tumultuous events which comprise it, have been well documented by historians and biographers since antiquity. No historian, ancient or contemporary, denies the important part Cicero played in the waning years of the Roman Republic, and many credit his eloquence as a force in his advancement and impact. The Roman historian Suetonius records that Augustus himself acknowledged the importance of Cicero in the shaping of events and encouraged his grandchildren to study the life and works of a man who seems to have opposed the chief features that came to represent the Augustan Principate.

Preface

Despite his well-chronicled life and the hundreds of private letters Cicero left to reveal a personality in more depth than any other individual in the ancient world, the forces that brought Cicero into prominence and (importantly) into power still want for further examination. Studies of the Roman Republic have understandably, and often accurately, examined the social, political, and economic forces shaping the calamitous period. As one among several prominent figures, Cicero could be swept easily into the generalizations that account for much of those happenings. Yet Cicero is not an individual who lends himself easily to generalizations. His uniqueness among other important figures of the period, his source of power, and his force in the Republic derived from his rhetorical ability. Thus, to study Cicero devoid of a sensitive understanding of his talents in rhetoric is to fundamentally misaccount the basis for his influence and, in a larger sense, to understand imprecisely the enormous importance rhetoric had in the social life of Republican Rome.

To favor Cicero's ability to express himself with a few platitudes about his eloquence is to move us only slightly toward a better understanding of his ability and force in Rome. Scholars of ancient history and rhetoric share agreement that Cicero was eloquent, but it is the nature of that talent and how it was applied that will reveal his impact. Much of our understanding of Cicero centers on his rhetoric, yet only recently has our knowledge of rhetoric—classical and contemporary—been sufficiently developed to allow an examination of how Cicero's use of rhetoric contributed to his achievements. Part of what constitutes the "new rhetorics" of the twentieth century is a sensitivity to classical rhetoric beyond mere philology to the social and contextual forces which influenced discourse and the epistemology of those individuals who articulated their thoughts and sentiments. Sensitivity to audience, the constraints of one's culture, the relationships between orality and literacy—these are the issues which inspire the essays in this volume and which warrant not merely "another look" at Cicero but a re-vision through perspectives which provide the most accurate rendering of this influential advocate.

Cicero's legal rhetoric might appear to be an odd source for revealing the relationship of his rhetoric to his society. The legal arguments are the realm of this inquiry for several reasons: they occur throughout much of Cicero's public career; they are focused on specific issues; they emerge from a discipline which has well-articulated procedures that serve as a point of reference; and they offer the opportunity to compare his extensive theoretical statements with actual arguments. Access to, let alone influence in, political life of Rome was guarded and conservative. Yet for Cicero the courts were an arena which was immediately accessible for rhetorical display. Moreover, issues of justice bore directly on social consequences and thus attracted a wide and engaged audience. In short, the courts became a source for social and political advancement. While the study of Roman law is a technical field unto itself, legalistic features are tangential to the inquiry. Fine points of the law will not account for Cicero's ability and are not underscored here except to illustrate his techniques in argument. Rather, his ability to compose discourse which transcended the specific case and technical points of jurisprudence, his opportunism in using the courts as a basis for social commentary, will be highlighted.

The chief feature grounding this inquiry is the relationship between Cicero's oratorical skills as an advocate and the compositional skills he demonstrated in the eventual publication of essays cast as his oral arguments for trials. Cicero's literate ability influenced both his oral presentation and the subsequently published versions of his speeches. The nature, features, and degree of that influence—as well as its implications for historians of rhetoric concerned with the relationship between orality and literacy—constitute the substance of this book. While a separate volume could be written on Ciceronian scholarship alone, works which focus on the social context and relationships between the oral and literate features of Cicero's legal argument would constitute meager entries. Much of traditional Ciceronian scholarship is philological in aim and disposition. Such studies "freeze" the writing of Cicero, creating a vacuum which isolates grammatical features or rhetorical figures but does little to place the discourse within the influences of its social context. Other studies discuss Cicero's orations and writings within a social context but do not offer a cognitive basis for analysis. Social history is presented on a general level at the expense of understanding the cognitive forces directing thought to real audiences. Cicero became a force in Roman society because of his rhetorical abilities, but the first arena for that ability was the law courts of Rome. Only after Cicero had established himself as Rome's preeminent advocate was he able to ascend the *cursus honorum* to a level that would make him a force in shaping his society. This book examines Cicero's ability as an advocate; his skills in oral argument, the techniques he used to influence listeners, the training which he so ardently applied in the pragmatics of heated debate, and his mastery in composing written argument will be topics of emphasis.

That Cicero used his ability in litigation as a source of political power in Roman is an historical fact. Yet as this inquiry reveals, the immediate power he earned through his oratorical ability became permanently fixed in Western civilization when he penned his speeches for mass distribution. In a society and profession dominated by oral discourse, Cicero was the first advocate to evidence a literate mind. Building on a tradition of distributing texts of speeches, Cicero transformed that practice by becoming the first literary figure of legal rhetoric of his period. Far from transcriptions, his "texts" became compositions which so vividly captured the robustness of the actual event that they endured as classics for generations and cultures that followed. It is this blend of the cognitive and social, the immediacy of oral discourse and the enduring characteristics of his compositions which provide the parameters for inquiry. This book examines the pragmatics of forensic argument; it is an effort to reconstruct the rhetorical techniques used in the courts and eventually in the culture. The reader may be enriched by a deeper understanding of the spirit of the actual deliberations and the force of Cicero's literate mind both in the preparation of oral argument and in the posttrial written compositions which were directed toward public audiences.

The efforts bound within these covers represent work done over a seventeen-year period. My earliest interest began in graduate school at Indiana University and resulted in a series of essays that served as preliminary versions of this work. These essays are listed in the Bibliography. Chapter 4, "Audiences of Cicero's Rhetoric," is a revision of an earlier essay I coauthored with Jeanne McClaran, a former graduate student with whom I worked when I was on the faculty at The University of Michigan. I thank her for her permission to expand upon our earlier efforts in a way that permitted this chapter to be included in the volume. I also wish to thank my colleagues at Carnegie Mellon University who continually introduce me to new ways of thinking about rhetoric, particularly Linda Flower, John R. Hayes, David Kaufer, Erwin Steinberg, and my dear friend Richard Young. I especially wish to thank my colleague A. Fred Sochatoff who reminds me continually of the benefits of humanism and of being humane. I have been blessed with mentors who have encouraged my best efforts: Bruce Loebs, Hal Barrett, J. Jeffery Auer, Raymond Smith, Robert Gunderson, Dennis Gouran, and Richard Johannesen. Likewise, I shall never be able to repay the kindnesses of Everett Lee Hunt, Harry Caplan, Wilbur Samuel Howell, Don Ochs, Ed Corbett, and James Kinneavy. The fine work of Kenney Withers, Dan Gunter, Natalia Nadraga, and Sally Master at Southern Illinois University Press all helped to sharpen the point of this book; I appreciate their insights and support. I especially wish to thank my ever-patient friend and secretary, Peggy Brucker, who coped with all my anxieties. To all that I have forgotten to mention, as the Roman prayer goes, I offer equal gratitude with those who are here remembered.

The Literate Mode of Cicero's Legal Rhetoric

1

The Pragmatics of the Roman Court

Cicero's [letters] sound far more oratorical, for one thing: the reader is felt in a more oral-aural way.

Walter J. Ong, Interfaces of the Word

Marcus Tullius Cicero is one of the rare individuals in Roman history who acquired fame as both a practitioner and theorist of rhetoric. In fact, he is more precisely considered an orator, rather than a rhetorician writing on rhetoric, for the theories he advanced in such works as *De Oratore* and *Orator* were heard first in the the courts and Forum before they were recorded for posterity. Yet Cicero was a great orator because of his ability to write, and versions of his legal speeches were composed for public distribution. Cicero was an expert in rhetorical composition, and the written accounts of his orations—however far they may have been from the actual utterances during the trials—are the preserved artifacts of his talent. The other dimension of his talent—one largely ignored by researchers—was his ability to compose "orations" which preserved the dynamic features of spontaneous oral discourse. We are tempted to view these orations as mere transcriptions of his oratory, but such a perspective distorts understanding and masks differences between the wranglings of litigation and the later artistic compositions offered in the form of orations. Mastery of a writing style which re-creates the characteristics of rhetorical situations reveals a tremendous resource of talent. The products of such efforts yield discourse which gives the appearance of transcribing events but, in reality, creates compositions which themselves stand as sustained arguments articulated to generations of audiences.

The permanence of written composition over the spoken word was a source of social power for Cicero. The popularization of his oral compositions not only attracted widespread interest but powerful clients who recognized the influence Cicero's oral and written skills could have in Rome. Thus, determining how Cicero emerged as such a powerful force in rhetoric and law as well as in the party politics of the Republic will reveal much about his talents and how they were applied. A simple explanation of this relationship would be accession through the *cursus honorum* or a standard progression of offices in which a few prominent individuals rose to the heights of Roman society. A more meaningful task is to determine how he was able to ascend so rapidly and attain such heights. A more complex and accurate explanation rests with an understanding of his proficiency in both oral argument and rhetorical composition directed toward legal and (eventually) public audiences.

There were three traditional qualifications which aided a young Roman in acquiring political power in the Republic: wealth, an aristocratic heritage, and military sagacity. Lacking these, Cicero utilized one further avenue of success: the power of forensic rhetoric.[1] Through his skill as a forensic orator, Cicero established a reputation and earned the political support that would allow him to become the first nonaristocrat (*novus homo*) to be elected consul in approximately thirty years.[2] In order to appreciate the relationship between forensic rhetoric and its pragmatic application as a source of power in Roman society, it is first necessary to understand the nature of the courts of Rome as well as Cicero's training and career.

The courts during the Roman Republic were strongly influenced by political and social forces. Almost fifty years before Cicero's birth, the tribune Lucius Calpurnius Piso Frugi secured the enactment of his *Lex Pecuniis Repetundis* (149 B.C.) which firmly established a court for extortion cases (*questio*). The standing commission for this court was entrusted to the Senate, which was greatly influenced by the *nobiles* or patricians. Two decades later, however, the famous popular leader Gaius Gracchus sponsored his *Lex Iudiciaria*, which shifted the control of the courts away from the Senate to the wealthiest nonpatrician class, the *equites*. This transfer of power between social classes not only shifted control of the courts but intensified already strained relations between the patrician-dominated Senate and the *equites*, a condition which lasted well into Cicero's legal career.[3] Such tumultuous events meant that the courts were a constantly changing audience and that each trial was presented in ever-changing social constraints. Several of Cicero's arguments reveal a sensitivity to the composition of listeners and the political forces which stood ready to interpret the larger social implications of the trial. Thus, both the original speeches and the later published versions of them were composed for volatile and changing audiences, a condition which compelled sensitivity.

It would be difficult to overstate these political constraints on legal argument. Even during Cicero's childhood, the courts were being manipulated by party politics. Quintus Servilius Caepio, consul in 196 B.C., passed a compromise law which provided for juries composed of senators and *equites*. About 101 B.C., the orator Gaius Servius Glaucia helped enact a law restoring the *repetundae* court and the quaestorship to the *equites*. Further reforms were attempted in 91 B.C. when the tribune Livius Drusus attempted to elevate three hundred *equites* to the Senate, and in c. 89 B.C. by the tribune Marcus Silvanus Platius, who introduced a *Lex Iudiciaria* which promoted mixed rather than equestrian juries. Certainly, efforts at reform were made, but such changes only dramatized the political and social implications of legal argument. One of the most significant reforms of the courts came during the early years of Cicero's career, when Sulla's conservative revolution and legislative programs of 81 B.C. returned the power of the six hundred members by promoting *equites* who supported him. Sulla delegated all the *questiones* to the senators. The institution of Sullan reform gave the Senate exclusive right to supply juries and control over at least seven permanent *questiones* which covered all major crimes: murder and poisoning, forgery, extortion, treason, electoral bribery, peculation, and assault.[4]

Later reforms modified Sulla's conservative reform of the courts. Lucius Aurelius, praetor in 70 B.C., tempered Sulla's legal reforms by passing the *Lex Aurelia Iudiciaria*, which allowed the juries of criminal courts to consist of an equal number of senators, *equites*, and *tribuni aerarii*, by creating three panels or *decuriae* of three hundred members each. The *tribuni aerarii* were citizens whose property qualifications were immediately below the Equestrian Order, and their affiliation was with the *equites* rather than the Senatorial Order. The *tribuni aerarii* were temporarily suppressed by Caesar, but while an active force, their support of the *equites* provided a two-thirds domination of the courts over the patricians of the Senate, which violated the spirit (if not the letter) of the Sullan reforms. During Cicero's legal career, factions of the Senate and *equites* continued to struggle for domination of the courts, which each group recognized as a source of political power. The influence of this struggle is apparent throughout Cicero's advocacy, for his career spanned the period from Sulla to Caesar and paralleled an era of transition in the power of legal oratory in the State and in the party politics of the courts. Preparing for a career in this tumultuous profession underscores the critical importance of rhetorical training.

Cicero's Education and Training in Forensic Rhetoric

Cicero's Rome was an "oral" society. The means of communication for social and political operation were assemblies where oral discourse could determine policy and shape events. Yet in a real sense Republican Rome was also a literate society. The distinguished authors that would crown the later Augustan Principate were beneficiaries of traditions of patronage established during the Republic. Public reading and recitation were common practices for the publication of civic and cultural matters. In short, the society, while understandably dominated by oral modes of expression, had integrated written discourse, even if its primary function was to facilitate and preserve oral discourse.

Little is known about the very early years of Cicero's education beyond Plutarch's statement that Cicero gained such a reputation as a young schoolboy that the fathers of other students came to observe his quickness and intelligence.[5] Cicero concentrated his scholastic talents on expression. He devoted his childhood efforts to poetic composition, which resulted in his early effort, *Pontius Glaucus*, and in voice training by the poet Aulus Lincinius Archias, whom he later defended in court.[6] While poetry is a natural genre for oral and written composition, Cicero's declamation became another source for refining oral and written skills. Cicero stated in the *Brutus* that as a youth he wrote, recited, and composed every day and in his *Tusculanae Disputationes* that he consistently declaimed more forensic orations (*controversiae*) than anyone else.[7] Evidently, Cicero continued this childhood practice throughout his legal career. According to Suetonius "Cicero actually declaimed in Greek all the way up to his praetorship, and as a rather old man, he declaimed in Latin with the consuls Hirtius and Pansa, whom he called his 'students' and 'big boys.'"[8] Cicero's ability to read, write, and speak Greek is important for understanding his rhetorical abilities. Being able to read Greek and having Demosthenes as his model for delivery and argument meant that Cicero "read" Demosthenes; that is, Cicero used his literate ability to understand Demosthenes' oratorical qualities. Toward the end of his legal career, Cicero wrote his *De Optimo Genere Oratorum*, which he claims to be a preface to his Latin translation of the speeches of Demosthenes and Aeschines.[9] Cicero was able to benefit from Demosthenes' oratory in the original Greek and eventually to use his literate skills to try to translate those benefits to his Latin readers. Such skills reveal a harmony between oral discourse and composition, a holistic approach to oral and written expression which Cicero nurtured throughout his career.

Writing speeches in preparation for oral presentation was popular in both Greece and Rome. Quintilian was fortunate enough to have access to Cicero's notes and mentioned that he frequently wrote out the most essential portions—particularly the opening remarks—beforehand and then invented subsequent lines of argument at the moment.[10] Cicero also used writing as a means of recording these spontaneous lines of argument. Plutarch believed that Cicero popularized the Greek method of shorthand composition in Rome and, with his freedman Tiro, developed a system of tachygraphy that permitted rapid recording of oral discourse.[11] It could be reasonably surmised that Tiro would record Cicero's oral arguments—doubtlessly to capture impromptu passages from the previously composed notes—and have the basic text for a polished posttrial composition.[12] Fully persuaded that writing was the greatest aid to effective oratory, Cicero believed that lack of motivation or ability and fear of criticism were the constraints that inhibited most orators from publishing their speeches.[13] Obviously, such shortcomings were not concerns for Cicero and other advocates who sought notoriety through publication.

Cicero remarked in his *Brutus* that Appius Claudius Caecus was the first advocate he knew to record his oral arguments for posterity.[14] The practice of recording fully developed orations for public distribution continued and became common among Roman advocates. Sensitive to the potential effect of his writing, Cicero was concerned about copyists who would draft inferior "pirate" texts. On one occasion Cicero wrote to his friend, Atticus, commenting on a circulating text of one of his speeches which he had neither written nor spoken![15] Cicero, however, revolutionized the custom and used the publication of his oral arguments as the opportunity to make a larger social statement, one that transcended the particulars of the case. Cicero's unique ability was in taking writing from this instrumental function as an aid to oral performance to a form of rhetorical expression in its own right. Cicero's public life and the methods he used to communicate offered no inducement to dissociate oral and written expression; his great talent was in recognizing and mastering legal composition. The route to such mastery, however, was grounded in oratory. Legal training was dominated and driven by proficiency in oral discourse. As a young man, Cicero expressed interest in becoming a student of Lucius Plotius Gallus, the famous founder of the first Latin rhetorical school in 95 B.C., but was dissuaded because of Gallus' reputation as a "barley-inflated" rhetorician, "puffed, light, and coarse."[16] Having rejected Gallus, Cicero initiated his training in forensic oratory by learning the theoretical intricacies of legal procedure from the younger Quintus Mucius Scaevola and the practical application of legal strategies from Quintus Hortenius Hortalus. Cicero mentioned that his father introduced him to Scaevola, the jurist, with the understanding "that, as long as I could and he permitted, I would never leave the old man's side."[17] Under Scaevola's guidance, Cicero memorized precepts and legal opinions with such commitment that he professed in *De Legibus* that he never seemed to be so absorbed in oratory as to turn away completely from civil law.[18] For practical experience in the Forum, however, Cicero "followed in the steps of Quintus Hortenius himself" since he "was considered first in pleading."[19]

Much of the early phase of Cicero's legal preparation stressed observation, imitation, and a mentor-apprentice relationship. Such methods are well suited to acquiring proficiency in orally dominated expression and, in fact, are similar to techniques of education for oral composition. Bards and rhapsodes frequently learned techniques of oral composition by modeling experts after intense, sustained observation, and Cicero appears to have done much the same in his legal preparation. Cicero was fortunate enough to enjoy a three-year period during his education where Rome, free from war, provided active courts for young orators to observe.[20] "At that time [81–80 B.C.]," wrote Cicero, "I first began to take private and public cases, not so that I could learn in the Forum, which several of my contemporaries did, but so that I could come into the Forum as educated as possible."[21] Cicero combined his legal training in the Forum with an emphasis in ethical philosophy, as he mentioned in his *De Natura Deorum*: "I did not begin to study philosophy suddenly or moderately. From my youth, I exhausted effort and care in that discipline, and even when it appeared negligible, I was actually studying philosophy extensively, which my orations, crammed with philosophical maxims, reveal; [as well as] the very learned friends who have always enriched my home, and the professors who gave me instruction—Diodotus, Philo, Antiochus, and Posidonius. In fact, if all the philosophical precepts are relevant to life, I think that I upheld those principles which reason and education dictate, both in my public and private matters."[22] When Cicero was very young, the Epicurean Phaedrus taught him philosophy but—as Aubrey Gwynn maintains—made little impression.[23] Yet, during the period after the three-year peace, when Cicero thought the courts had all but vanished, he turned "completely" to Philo, the head of the Academy, as well as to other Greek scholars who fled to Rome because of the Mithridatic War.[24]

At the age of twenty-six, Cicero decided to continue his education abroad after he had spoken in defense of Sextus Roscius in a property dispute with one of Sulla's henchmen, L. Cornelius Chrysogonus. During his two years abroad (79–77 B.C.), Cicero studied in Athens, Asia Minor, and Rhodes. He spent the first six months of his foreign studies in Athens, continuing his philosophical education under the *scholarchos* Antiochus, who emphasized the doctrines of the Old Academy.[25] While in Athens, Cicero combined the philosophical education obtained from Antiochus with rhetorical exercises under Demetrius, the Syrian, whom he described as "a long standing and not obscure teacher of oratory."[26]

In Asia, where the predominant rhetorical tradition emphasized the sort of embellishment criticized by Dionysius of Halicarnassus as "replete with petty artifices, ignoble, [and] nonvirile," Cicero studied under Menippus of Stratonicae, whom he considered "the most eloquently eminent orator in all Asia at the time."[27] Cicero studied under other rhetorical scholars of Asia Minor who are now little more than names to us—Dionysius of Magnesia, Aeschylus of Cnidus, and Xenocles of Adramyttium. One of Cicero's most beneficial experiences, however, came from his education in Rhodes when he studied under Apollonius Molo. Cicero believed Molo's skill as a pleader, logographer, and teacher helped temper his own excessively flamboyant style.[28]

Cicero's Hellenistic education exposed him to two important features of rhetorical instruction which facilitated his ability in the composition of oral argument. His Greek education provided training in logography, exposing him to the process of speech composition that had been refined for about four centuries. Second, Cicero was instructed in Greek declamation, which was markedly different than Roman declamation.[29] Roman declamation stressed oral argument; in fact, it was a standard feature of legal training. Greek declamation, which was less accessible to other Roman advocates, stressed written composition skills and actively instituted such principles as *stasis* as part of the exercises. Thus, Cicero had the benefits of logography and Greek declamation to draw on when he composed his legal orations and had, by his own accounts, benefited greatly from such training in an integrated writing-speaking approach.

Cicero returned to Rome holding strong opinions on the objectives of the forensic career which he was about to renew and on the tenets of his rhetorical education which he hoped to apply to the law courts and his political career. He later expressed these sentiments in *De Oratore*: "Oratory ought to be directed out of this private and cloistral exercise [and] into the pubic mainstream, into the arena, into the clamor, into the camp, and into forensic debate; everything must be employed and risked to the strength of her talent. In short, imprisoned meditation ought to be brought into the light of truth." [30] A survey of Cicero's preparation for the courts demonstrates that whatever natural ability and practical experience he may have possessed was complemented by an uncommonly comprehensive education in such areas as poetry, philosophy, law, and literature, as well as a thorough training in rhetoric and oratory. After his training, Cicero, like many ambitious young Romans, sought political power through a uniform progression of elected offices or *cursus honorum*: questorship, praetorship, consulship, and censorship. Yet, whether a young Roman was a *nobilis*, whose admission to the Senate was assured by his heritage, or a municipal *novus homo* ("new man") such as Cicero, the acquisition of strong support was essential for any appreciable degree of political success. Cicero acquired support by offering his services in forensic oratory, establishing a network of influential patrons, clients, and friends who provided the necessary support.

Cicero's Forensic Oratory and Political Advancement

Cicero recognized that his talent in oral argument could be used efficiently in the courts. Yet while proficiency in oral discourse could earn Cicero immediate victories and a word-of-mouth reputation, no artifacts of his talent would endure to sustain this reputation. Composing forensic rhetoric after the trial provided enduring evidence that continually enhanced Cicero's reputation. After the current interest surrounding a trial and its issues waned, the published orations remainded visible and included legal accounts of a trial as well as commentaries on social and political conditions. In time, the "text" of Cicero's forensic compositions changed as the context changed so that the essays came to be viewed less as legal documents and more as vehicles for social commentary and political advancement. Thus, Cicero's proficiency in oral argument helped him acquire his reputation, and his composing skills helped him sustain it. Cicero's oral and written talents both served his political ends.

A brief account of Cicero's advocacy underscores the importance of his oral and written forensic skills in the politics of Roman society. In fact, Cicero's own attitude toward political advancement illustrates the impact which he felt forensic rhetoric had on his political career. In 75 B.C., at the earliest legal age, Cicero was elected quaestor for a one-year term in western Sicily. One of the primary benefits which he felt this office gave him was the right to express his opinions in the Senate.[31] Furthermore, through such early defense cases as his *Pro Quinctio* and *Pro Roscio Amerino*, his successful prosecution of the proconsul Gaius Verres in 70 B.C., and his deliberative orations against Catiline in 63 B.C., Cicero established himself as a leading advocate and politician in Rome. Partially through his oratorical ability, he earned the distinction of breaking into the strict aristocratic circle established by Sulla, becoming the first *novus homo* to be elected consul in three decades.[32]

The contribution of oratory to Cicero's legal and political career was best summarized by his brother, Quintus, who emphasized that "whoever you are, you are from this."[33] Besides believing that oratory had always exercised great influence, Cicero professed an elitist position on the qualifications of a rhetor.[34] "Out of all those individuals who have undertaken very liberal studies and instruction," he wrote, "a small number of outstanding poets and orators have stood out."[35] Cicero believed that "everyone had an interest in speaking," but that the qualifications for successful oratory were so stringent that it was easier to become a general than an accomplished pleader.[36] In essence, Cicero felt he had to compensate for his lack of nobility.[37] Accordingly, he developed his ability as an advocate so that he could establish a *clientelae* that would advance him politically.

Cicero recognized that politics had a definite impact on the court, an impact which often resulted in judicial corruption. The oligarchical control of the courts by patricians excluded the voice of the populace, and since the leading political offices were dominated by these *nobiles*, politics blended unchecked with the courts resulted in corruption. A clear example of such corruption came in Cicero's youthful defense of Sextus Roscius in 80 B.C. Cicero remarked that he was virtually the only orator courageous enough to risk Sulla's displeasure and undertake the defense.[38] The primary reason for the unpopularity of the case was the prosecution being offered by the colleagues of Sulla, who was then in his second consulship. The fear of the jurors that a verdict against one of Sulla's men could be taken personally by the consul was so strong that Cicero had to devote part of his case to reminding them of their obligations to justice.[39] In spite of the intimidation by the prosecution, Cicero was able to win the case by carefully incriminating Sulla's men while praising Sulla himself.[40]

By the time of Cicero's prosecution of the infamous proconsul Gaius Verres in 70 B.C., the corruption of the Senatorial courts had greatly increased. Despite Verres' considerable influence within the patrician class and the oratorical brilliance of his advocate Hortensius, Cicero was able to secure a charge of extortion from the aristocratic jury. Cicero indicated throughout the prosecution that this case was not only a trial of Verres, but of the fitness of the Senatorial Order to engage in court management. Sulla's conservative reforms had removed the fifty-year control of the law courts from the Equestrian Order, but the Senate was hard-pressed to match the reputation for fairness that the Equestrian Order had earned. Cicero urged the senators to invoke their power and "blot out and remove the disgrace and infamy taken on by this Order through the years" or else risk having men continue to think "that a completely different Order [Equestrian] for judging matters ought to be sought."[41] Cicero's purpose was to have his senatorial jurors believe that the entire revamping of the courts hinged on the outcome of this trial, and he even emphasized that Pompey and the *Populares* already had enough force to change the jury composition to represent levels of Roman citizenship.[42] In essence, Cicero realized the need for an honest jury, since it would determine "whether in the case of this man it can be established that a very criminal and very wealthy individual can be condemned by a senatorial court."[43] Cicero's strategy was to convince the judges of the discredit which all senators would share by acquitting a known criminal.

Cicero continued to enhance his forensic and political reputation after the Verrine orations and moved through his *cursus honorum* to the consulship in 63 B.C. During this seven year period, the rising power of the *Populares* held increasing importance to Caesar, Pompey, and Crassus. The courts were not freed from the factions, which continued to fight for supremacy. The Ciceronian ideal of a stable court functioning in a tranquil state faced a major challenge: the conspiracy of Catiline. Catiline, who was tolerated if not supported by Caesar and Crassus, was defeated by Cicero in the consular elections and organized a conspiracy which Cicero suppressed. As a patrician and former Sullan supporter, Catiline might have transferred the power of the courts back to the Senatorial Order if his takeover had been successful. Cicero himself admitted in 63 B.C. that the courts were disorganized and vulnerable to the kind of strong-arm reform that had occurred two decades earlier.[44] Furthermore, Cicero maintained in his *Paradoxa Stoicorum* that the law courts were all but nonexistent when the State was torn apart by the conspiracy because the laws lacked force and the courts were corrupted.[45] Consequently, Cicero believed that his efforts against Catiline had preserved the stability of the State and allowed the courts to function in a climate of justice and equity.[46] Such action earned Cicero the esteem and *vir bonus* image imperative for political advancement.

The suppression of the Catilinarian conspiracy, however, did not thwart other forces attempting to seize control and misuse the courts as a means of gaining political power. Cicero's personification of the abuse of forensic oratory was Publius Clodius Pulcher. In May 61 B.C., Cicero presented convincing evidence that Clodius had violated the sanctity of the *Bona Dea* festival. When Clodius was narrowly acquitted by the jury which Crassus had bribed, Cicero wrote to Atticus, "immediately after the acquittal of Clodius, I observed the frivolity and weakness of the courts."[47] He became increasingly disenchanted with the political climate and wrote to Atticus again in 59 B.C., saying "I . . . attend no public affairs and direct all my work and effort to my forensic duty."[48] When Cicero's advocacy was interrupted by his exile in 58 B.C.—an exile which was secured through Clodius' tribuneship—the juries pronounced no verdicts.[49] Corruption was, at best, only suspended, for Cicero's letters of 54 B.C. provide a disappointing testimony to the renewed activity of the courts where more than one trial of *praevaricatio*, or fraudulent mismanagement of a case, occurred.[50]

After his return from exile, Cicero continued his forensic activity, observing that the Forum was unusually peaceful.[51] He believed, however, that this tranquility was actually "more civil senility than acquiescence," and that its probable cause was the emergence of a dictatorship.[52] By October 54 B.C., Cicero had resigned himself to believing that there were really no more Republic, Senate, or law courts, although he was active in the courts that year, winning his case for Vatinius and losing his defense of Gabinius. Cicero's last major forensic effort prior to the Civil War of 52 B.C. was his unsuccessful defense of Milo, who was impeached for the murder of Clodius. During the prelude to the Civil War, the traditional sources of power were being consolidated under a few individuals and eventually became embodied under one dynast: Gaius Julius Caesar.

Cicero had mixed opinions concerning the courts under Caesar. In letters to his friends, he made no secret of his sorrow over the loss of the Republic and admitted to one colleague that "nothing is more dear to me than the Republic herself."[53] In his *De Republica*, Cicero argued that man was in concord through speech and that it was the right of the people to be masters of the laws and courts.[54] To Cicero, Caesar's control of the courts fell far short of this ideal. There was some indication that Cicero initially believed Caesar might use his power to stabilize the courts after the bloodshed of the Civil War, and the court cases judged by Caesar (*Pro Ligario* and *Pro rege Deiotaro*) reinforce the impression of his idealism.[55] Cicero soon realized, however, that Caesar used the courts to further his own political ends. A letter to Atticus explaining his responses to a plea from a relative of Caesar to defend him indicated Cicero's embitterment: "I replied to him that he had no need for a counsel, since Caesar, a relative of his, was all-powerful; nevertheless, I am going to support him."[56]

After the death of Caesar, Cicero discovered that such men as Mark Anthony so thoroughly attempted to corrupt the courts that he recommended they be closed.[57] Disillusioned, embittered, and believing that the courts were abolished in all but name, Cicero sought retirement from forensic oratory: "For seeing that it wearied me earlier, when age and ambition motivated me, and I was in short, permitted not to defend whom I did not wish to defend; but at this time life is of no account. Actually, I do not anticipate any reward for my effort, and I feel that I am compelled to defend a number of men, whose merits do not deserve my best efforts, at the request of those who have merited well. And so in my judgment, I seek at last every reason for living as I see fit."[58] Cicero's death by proscription not only ended the life of one of Rome's most famous advocates, but also represented the end of Republican forensic oratory.

Cicero's life is a testimonial to resourcefulness. Denied access to many of the traditional sources of power in Roman society, Cicero created his own. He utilized his compositional skills to produce legal orations which became the medium for his political advancement, catapulting him to the forefront of political life. There is no doubt that Cicero was sensitive to the power that forensic rhetoric had on Roman society. In an age when advocates were tempted to compromise ethical standards for political expediency and when charges of bribery and corruption (*maiestas*) were common, Cicero praised the legal profession as the foundation of divinely guided practical wisdom which ordered Rome.[59] In his *De Officiis*, he portrayed forensic orators as guardians of the civil law whose obligation was to maintain the tranquility of the State.[60] This commitment to public service was ascribed by the ancients to the chief rank of civil professions.[61] "Favors and patronage are extensively accessible therefore to an eloquent man," wrote Cicero, "when he genuinely works and when, in accordance with ancient practices, he assumes the defense cases of many with seriousness and gratitude."[62]

Cicero saw eloquence as the force which bound society, and the establishment of law as the force which sustained this unity and allowed Romans to recognize order in their existence.[63] The obligation of sustaining legal order in the society was delegated to the forensic orator. The role of forensic activity, however, was not to establish tranquility in society, but rather to sustain it. "For indeed," Cicero maintained, "the desire for speaking is not customarily waged, or when hindered and bound by the tyranny of a king; eloquence is the follower of peace and the ally of leisure and, in an already well-ordered state, a sort of foster-child."[64] Oratory was not only prestigious and popular after peace had been attained, but could exist only when questions of justice were resolved in the courts and not on the battlefield.[65]

Cicero's belief about the limitation of forensic rhetoric prompts an evaluation of his concepts of justice and equity. To Cicero, justice (*iustitia*) was most often manifested in the advocate by his attempts to attain equity (*aequitas*), the aim of the courts.[66] Both equity and justice are terms which Cicero used to indicate a condition of balance or tranquility. The objective of litigation was the attainment of equity, to readjust an imbalance through an interpretation of existing laws on a particular issue. Justice, however, implied a far more generic balance than the equity of individual cases; it was the virtuous condition of balance upon which a society was built. Nevertheless, a "just" orator who continually strove for equity within the courts was also contributing to the maintenance of moral balance for the State. In this respect, Ciceronian equity was also the foundation of statecraft and—along with justice, the highest virtue—was both the principal ingredient for making citizens "good men" (*viri boni*) and a strong factor in promoting and strengthening society.[67]

Justice and equity were elements in Cicero's supreme law: reason.[68] In essence, Cicero's law was the natural intelligence of man which provided the basis for a just society; ignorance, or man's failure in natural intelligence, necessitated the reinstatement of equity through litigation.[69] One task of the advocate, then, was to interpret the conditions of a case to his listeners. Because of the need for listener understanding, the pleader occasionally sacrificed eloquence for the sake of clarifying reason.[70]

Despite his idealization of justice, however, Cicero recognized that justice could not be considered an end in itself.[71] The "favor" (*iucunditas*) which a just orator elicited was the basic virtue which allowed him to be considered a "good man" (*vir bonus*) in the eyes of his audience. Thus, the concept of being morally just was not an ideal without a practical referent, but rather a means of gaining honorable distinction (*gloria*) through the *vir bonus* character. In Cicero's concept of forensic rhetoric, then, law, justice, and equity could not only serve as guardians of social values and keepers of the peace, but also provided the practical reward of public recognition which often lead to more power within the

State. From this perspective, published compositions of forensic arguments became benchmarks, paradigms for political and social conduct. While Cicero's oral skills won many cases, his forensic compositions transcended the particular and became generalized statements about social issues and values.

Summary

This chapter stresses four topics important for understanding subsequent discussions of Cicero's forensic rhetoric. First, Cicero's extensive legal training reveals a thorough preparation in oral and written composition and a sensitivity to the respective advantages they could offer in Roman society. Second, various political factions recognized the advantage of controlling the courts and fought for domination prior to and throughout Cicero's career. In fact, Cicero's career as an advocate paralleled an era of transition in the courts of Rome, spanning the dynasts from Sulla to Caesar and a struggle between the Senatorial and Equestrian Orders for judicial control. The third item is of major significance as a starting point of the study: forensic rhetoric was a source of political power whereby young Romans who secured legal victories for influential clients achieved public offices. Cicero, a *novus homo*, lacking noble birth, military talent, and wealth—the conventional sources of power for political advancement—concentrated his effort in forensic rhetoric and gained enough success to secure the consulship in 63 B.C. Fourth and last, Cicero believed that oratory is the force that binds a society and aids in maintaining an already-existing tranquil state but does not create a peaceful state out of discord. Cicero also maintained that justice and equity, aspects of the supreme law of reason, were parts of a conceptual method of resolving human failure in man's otherwise natural intelligence. Failure in man's natural intelligence resulted in ignorance and necessitated litigation in order to resolve conflict by acquiring knowledge. Furthermore, Cicero maintained that justice was not an end in itself but a method for preserving a stable society and a means of gaining popular favor for the advocate, the image of the *vir bonus*. Writing and publishing his legal orations then served not only his political advancement but, ideally, sustained harmony by preserving opinions about social conduct.

The *rhetorica* of such successful orators as Cicero were important because they provided guidelines for political advancement. However, this source of power was changed with the Roman revolution, which transformed the Republic into the monarchial Principate of Augustus. Cicero's works were no longer used as a practical tool for political advancement in a free society, but rather as literate guidelines for such State propagandists as Virgil, Horace, and Livy. Yet the impact Cicero had on forensic rhetoric, and the standards he established, were the result of a tradition of forensic rhetoric of which he was a beneficiary.

2

The Benefactors of Forensic Discourse

Cicero . . . often imitated models . . . and saw crises in which he found parallels from earlier events in Roman history.
Cecil W. Wooten, Cicero's *Philippics* and Their Demosthenic Model: The Rhetoric of Crisis

While Cicero is commonly acknowledged as the preeminent advocate of the Republic, there is little doubt that he held many of his predecessors and contemporaries in high esteem. The *Brutus* is a testimonial to the high standards of eloquence attained by earlier orators. His characterization of influential Roman advocates as dialogue participants in his treatises is invariably laudatory. While his contributions to rhetoric became a standard of excellence for his own period and for much of the discipline's history in the Latin-speaking West, there is little doubt that Cicero saw himself as a beneficiary of a long tradition of Roman forensic rhetoric. Cicero was like other advocates of his generation, who rooted their ability in a careful scrutiny of prominent advocates. Cicero's distinction from his contemporaries, however, is apparent in his sensitive observation of their strengths and weaknesses, and his ability to benefit from these observations was markedly different from other Roman advocates. Cicero received extensive training not only in oral argument but in composition, and he continued to perfect and apply his literary skills throughout his career. The superiority of Cicero's literate skills enabled him to bring to the courts modes of thought and expression which are less easily attained by orality alone. But before Cicero's unique abilities can be discussed, it is necessary to frame his oral and literate skills within the context of the Roman tradition of legal argument by synthesizing his own views on Roman advocacy and examining extant fragments of the orations of pre-Ciceronian advocates.

The rhetorical standards Cicero inherited are essentially unknown, but his perspective on the merits and shortcomings of previous advocates offers insight to the forces shaping his style of argument.[1] Several scholars of Roman rhetoric, such as A. D. Leeman, are concerned over the scanty knowledge of pre-Ciceronian orators in general, and S. F. Bonner notes that the lack of a "full literary account" means that an important period has been "unduly neglected."[2] Attempts to gather information on pre-Ciceronian forensic rhetoric reveal only limited contributions.[3] There are, however, works which provide a basic understanding of this period by treating it as one era in the general history of rhetoric, although they lack the necessary detailed analysis.[4] A more serious obstacle is the inclination to accept unchallenged and isolated comments from such works as *De Oratore*, *Brutus*, and *Orator*. The temptation is understandable since Cicero remains the most influential advocate of the Roman Republic as well as the most prolific scholar of Latin rhetoric. Nevertheless, if there is one point upon which researchers of classical rhetoric agree, it is that Cicero frequently wrote and spoke out of expediency and deviated from his theoretical precepts on forensic rhetoric in his own practice as an advocate.

Written texts were important in the study of model advocates. Cicero's comments reveal that copies of speeches were common sources for study but were not always available in any systematic way. In one instance, Cicero wrote to his brother, Quintus, bragging that no one would read his opponent's speech but that schoolboys would commit his to memory.[5] Written texts frequently incorporated techniques to simulate oral style. Cicero's rhetorical treatises, for example, are cast in dialogue fashion with a theme anchoring the contrived discussion. Features of oral discourse in written composition capture the liveliness and familiarity of oral communication. Proficiency in such writing skills transcends mere description, requiring a sensitivity to effective oral presentation and a knowledge of how to transfer such characteristics to writing. Thus, Cicero's education included not only observing great orators but also reading them and recognizing the importance and difficulty of transferring oral features to written documents. Coming from the most prominent beneficiary of this educational tradition, Cicero's observations on these advocates (and their texts) are as important as a careful examination and synthesis of the fragments. Perhaps the most valuable source of accurate information on the period is the relevant commentary from Cicero's orations, philosophical treatises, letters, *rhetorica*, and poetry.

As a reading of the *Brutus* reveals, there were no fewer than two hundred prominent orators in the five generations which preceded Cicero. Scores of these speakers enjoyed such brief fame that they were as little known to Cicero's contemporaries as they are today. The task is to select and examine those advocates who had the greatest influence on the Republic and, specifically, on the courts as viewed by Cicero, since it is his perception which provides the index for understanding who influenced him and what traits he most admired. A careful synthesis of his comments will be a route to understanding the features he considered effective in forensic rhetoric.[6]

The age of pre-Ciceronian forensic rhetoric corresponds to the "pre-classical" age of Roman law; that is, the systematization and stabilization of law and society characteristic of the Augustan Principate were already being established during and before the age of Cicero.[7] But prior to the age of Augustus and certainly prior to the age of Cicero, the provinces of law and politics were far less discrete. The courts were the arena for the structure and maintenance of Roman values, but they also served as a forum for public articulation of political positions. Cicero's own career—and no doubt the careers of many advocates who came before him—clearly reveals how proficiency in forensic rhetoric could greatly enhance political advancement.

The advocates who preceded Cicero personify and articulate values during a period we would otherwise know little about. The process of abstracting qualities from models was a common practice in Roman education and a major aspect of Cicero's rhetorical training.[8] In studying jurisprudence with the Augur Quintus Mucius Scaevola and in following the steps of Quintus Hortensius Hortalus, Cicero was taking the common course of synthesizing the precepts and emulating the style of successful advocates.[9] Lacking an advanced training procedure, the only source for a practical education in forensic rhetoric was the study of model cases and advocates—an education by historical precedent. Therefore, one method of understanding the rhetoric of the Republic is to observe the advocates Cicero praised and the qualities they possessed. Once these traits have been isolated, they can serve as the standard for Cicero's forensic rhetoric.

The Consummate Advocates: Lucius Licinius Crassus and Marcus Antonius

Lucius Licinius Crassus and Marcus Antonius were two Roman advocates who most closely personified Cicero's ideal speakers.[10] Crassus and Antonius, who established themselves a generation before Cicero, so developed the art of eloquence that their era has been considered the beginning of the golden age of Roman oratory.[11] Because of their ability, Cicero believed that "Latin oratory shared equal fullness with the glory of the Greeks."[12] Their clients also recognized their oratorical abilities, for Crassus and Antonius deliberated on the most important cases, and "on this point, all men agreed: no one who would use one of these men would need the talent of any other advocate."[13]

If Cicero were compelled to choose who was the foremost advocate, the distinction would rest with Crassus. Through his dialogue characters, Antonius and Scaevola, Cicero frequently praised Crassus as a man of vast natural ability (*ingenium*) who possessed a strong desire to learn (*studium acies*) and who committed himself completely to his profession (*industria superior*).[14] Through the character Scaevola, Cicero noted Crassus as the most knowledgeable orator he had known, calling him "godlike" (*deus*) in eloquence.[15] Cicero's personal view was more tempered than that of his characters in *De Oratore*. He considered Crassus an orator who approached the highest level of perfection yet needed to increase his knowledge of philosophy, civil law, and history and may have been guilty of "more copiousness than oratorical sagacity."[16] Nevertheless, Cicero's regard for Crassus was well known, and he would not hesitate to cite a case of Crassus' as a precedent in his own deliberations.[17] Cicero's opinion is clearly stated in the *Brutus*: "Although I indeed attribute as many qualities to Antonius as I earlier mentioned, nevertheless I consider nothing could have been more finished than [the eloquence of] Crassus."[18]

Outside of Cicero's works and letters, little is known about Lucius Licinius Crassus. His speeches were rare even during Cicero's time; as he indicates in the *Orator*: "There are very few orations of Crassus' and none are forensic orations."[19] Today only fragments of Crassus' speeches exist, and the major source for his style of oratory is derived from Cicero's comments in the *Brutus* and *De Oratore*.[20] Cicero's lament over the inaccessibility of written copies of Crassus' legal arguments is revealing. His remarks clearly indicate that copies were available and that such copies were seen as models for serious study. Obviously, however, the distribution of copies was limited, even for an advocate as revered as Crassus. Cicero's sensitivity to the importance of written texts—their diverse and enduring value—is readily apparent.

Crassus must have been an impressive orator. Catulus, upon hearing him speak was so moved that he insisted that all other orators "be given hay."[21] Crassus' main strength as an orator was his rapport with audiences, which may have been partly due to his unique blend of a brief but ornate style of oratory.[22] Other reasons for Crassus' success as an orator were his "outstanding sagacity" and exceptional wit.[23] Cicero greatly admired these traits, but was particularly impressed by Crassus' sincere commitment (*summa gravitas*) and by his peculiar devotion to deep meditation, which occasionally took hold of him during his trials![24] Another of Crassus' strengths was his ability to isolate and provide copious arguments for the central points of equity and justice in legal issues.[25] Cicero praised Crassus' precise Latin diction, meticulous preparation, restrained gestures, range of emotions, and unequaled proficiency in cross-examination.[26]

Marcus Antonius was the only orator who Cicero felt approached the excellence of Crassus. Both Antonius and Crassus engaged in great cases, but Antonius was more suited to the courts—probably "because Antonius, who was especially desired, readily undertook cases, while Crassus was more selective."[27] Cicero indicated that he was aware of no extant texts of speeches by Marcus Antonius, although some fragments do exist today.[28] If these fragments are a representative sampling of his pleadings, then Antonius undertook more defense than prosecution cases.[29]

Stylistically, Antonius differed from Crassus but possessed many qualities which Cicero praised. The primary quality was Antonius' *actio* or delivery, which by present-day standards would boarder on histrionics but which Cicero considered unique "both for creating faith and provoking pity."[30] Cicero recorded that on one occasion, "Antonius, when vigorously speaking on the Varian Law in his own behalf, touched the ground with his knee," and on another occasion he concluded his peroration by tearing open the tunic of his defendant to reveal his scars.[31] In essence, Antonius seems to have had the ability to excite his listeners with strong dramatic appeals. Antonius' animated style depended on presence; his physical and tonal gestures created an impression that the written text would be hard-pressed to duplicate. Just as a play loses its vitality when it is only read and not acted, so also would forensic rhetoric lack a vitality if it were merely composed as a transcription. Yet a composition which could capture the liveliness of Antonius' delivery would be alluring to an audience. Cicero's understanding of Antonius' presence in court underscored the importance of incorporating techniques which could enliven the written oration.

Antonius demonstrated other traits which earned Cicero's praise, the most notable of which was his apparent spontaneity. Cicero attributed this to his extraordinary memory and strong disapproval of schematic rhetoric.[32] Antonius "always seemed unprepared for speaking, but was actually so well prepared . . . that some judges seemed not to have taken care to have sufficiently prepared themselves."[33] Cicero indicated in *De Oratore* that he took great pains to represent Crassus and Antonius as accurately as possible.[34] If we can trust Cicero's portrayal of Antonius in *De Oratore*, he was insufficiently trained in the liberal arts and relied on a native faculty for pleading his cases.[35]

Cicero viewed both Crassus and Antonius as men of well-rounded ability, "for each was," he wrote, "not only superior to all in zeal, natural ability and education, but accomplished in his own style, so that this oratorical finish was neither lacking in Antonius nor overflowing in Crassus."[36] Cicero praised Crassus over Antonius for his desire to supplement natural talent with a rigorous and thorough education. Yet both Crassus and Antonius were praised for their personal character and style, for Cicero seemed to admire the Asiatic embellishment of Crassus as much as he did the Attic perspicuity of Antonius. Crassus' unique blend of somber severity and wit were as highly praised as Antonius' histrionics in delivery. Cicero emphasized that both men were also greatly admired by their listeners, and he held praise for each man's memory.

Praise for two dissimilar advocates indicates Cicero's perception of the traits of successful litigants. Cicero's comments on Crassus and Antonius demonstrate that he acknowledged no single ideal style of forensic rhetor. Cicero conceded that he preferred Crassus to Antonius, based on the merit of Crassus' language.[37] Nevertheless, in Cicero's opinion, both men surpassed all other orators, not because either of them had found the formula for oratory, but because both had discovered effective methods for a practical rhetoric. That is, both men possessed certain traits which they so developed and successfully applied in the courts and Forum that each approached a standard of excellence for Cicero. His observations also recognize the importance of written texts of orations and the value of conveying features of communication normally associated with the liveliness of oral argument.

Cicero's Rival and Hero: Quintus Hortensius Hortalus

Quintus Hortensius Hortalus was a successful forensic rhetor who practiced in the generation immediately following Crassus and Antonius, overlapping the legal career of Cicero. Although the career of Hortensius had a major impact on Roman forensic rhetoric, only fragments of his speeches survive, fragments which reveal over twenty actions for defense and no apparent prosecution speeches.[38] This surviving evidence, coupled with references to Hortensius in Cicero's orations, suggests that Hortensius emphasized defense in his legal career. Cicero notes in his *Brutus* that Hortensius' legal career began at age ninteen and lasted forty-four years, indicating that he retained cases until he was sixty-three years old.[39] Cicero also mentions, however, that, after Hortensius' consulship in 69 B.C., he lost his zeal for forensic oratory and did not renew his practice until after Cicero's own consulship in 63 B.C.[40]

Apparently, Hortensius practiced certain court strategies throughout his career that were not above reproach. E. G. Sihler suggests that Hortensius may have gained his reputation in forensic oratory by defeating *puri nobiles*, or inexperienced young patricians, and believes that Hortensius tried to establish Quintus Caecilius as a "straw man" prosecutor in the *Divinatio* for the Verres trial so that, as Verres' advocate, he could secure an easy victory.[41] Fragments of Cicero's lost treatise, *Hortensius*, indicate that Hortensius did not share complete agreement with Cicero on the benefits of uniting philosophy with rhetoric.[42] Despite this apparent difference of opinion, Cicero expressed an evaluation of Hortensius' attributes at the conclusion of his *De Oratore* through Crassus, who saw Hortensius as "an orator with very sharp natural ability, passionate zeal, an exceptional education, and an extraordinary memory."[43] Perhaps the most important of these qualities was his command of *memoria*. Cicero wrote that Hortensius' great natural gift was such "that he was able to recall, without aid, all that he thought and wrote as well as all of his opponents' arguments."[44] This unique memory aided Hortensius not only in retaining lines of arguments from his opponents' speeches, but also in recalling and amassing the commonplaces applicable to the issues.

An important relationship between orality and literacy emerges from Cicero's praise of Hortensius. Hortensius composed legal arguments beforehand and memorized them for oral delivery. Recall also Cicero's admiration for Antonius' apparently spontaneous delivery. Cicero recognized the importance of writing as a form of legal preparation—even if only as an aid to memory—and its value in capturing the tenor of spontaneous delivery. The relationship of oral and written composition is apparent here as a preparation to legal argument. Cicero's ability was in extending this relationship to published orations after the trial, in using the dimensions of writing and speaking to compose something much more complex than mere transcription.

Different oratorical styles imposed different demands on the composers. Cicero believed that Hortensius' style encompassed the best qualities of Asianism, but he also believed that Asianism was best suited to youth and not to mature advocates.[45] While young, Hortensius—with his emotional language and lively delivery—had an impact on the populace.[46] As a mature advocate, however, Hortensius continued to speak in his youthful style. The *gravitas* which earned Crassus popular approval was absent in Hortensius, who used an over-studied delivery and lacked "personal authority" (*auctoritas*).[47] Hellenic logographers were sensitive to the relationship between speech style and the presentation of one's person and called such a phenomenon *ethopoiia*, or the ability to compose discourse appropriate to the individual. Cicero's remarks about Hortensius and Antonius illustrate that the construction of a *persona* was vital to suasory discourse and a feature to consider in the composition of legal arguments.[48]

Technicians of Forensic Rhetoric: The Quinti Mucii Scaevolae and Servius Sulpicius Rufus

Certain advocates during Cicero's career placed strong emphasis on the techniques of jurisprudence. Cicero realized how difficult it was for an advocate to develop the breadth of practical rhetoric necessary for popular support and to be an expert in jurisprudence.[49] Furthermore, he believed that orators who emphasized jurisprudence often restricted themselves to a narrow interpretation of the principles of law. Less "technical" advocates, such as Crassus, Antonius, and Hortensius, aroused their listeners through a blend of reason and eloquence. Cicero was quite direct on this point: "For who will ever doubt that in our State eloquence always held first priority in peaceful matters, and jurisprudence second? Since obviously in the first there is a great deal of favor, glory, and protection; in the second, there is the instruction of prosecutors and bail-bond suits. Jurisprudence indeed often seeks aid from eloquence itself and, in fact, when opposed, can hardly defend its own sphere and aims."[50] Cicero believed that successful forensic advocates actually had more natural ability (*ingenium*) than legal education (*doctrina*) and thought that the role of giving legal advice was practical but trivial.[51] In *De Oratore*, Crassus and Antonius mocked this technical oratory as unimportant and irrelevant in cases where the law was beyond argument and clearly inferior to more effective devices such as wit and charm.[52] In short, Cicero maintained that *techniae rhetoricae* in advocacy ought to be limited "because knowledge is pleasing to men, but a schematic language is mistrusted."[53] Although Cicero de-emphasized the role of jurisprudence in litigation, there were certain fundamental traits which he praised and thought important in forensic rhetoric. Three of the more famous orators who stressed legal science and earned the praise of Cicero were the Quinti Mucii Scaevolae and Servius Sulpicius Rufus.

The Elder Scaevola exhibited two traits of forensic rhetoric which Cicero admired, possibly because they could be used for applying the concepts of justice and equity: a mastery of legal science and procedure and a strong moral character. Cicero believed that the Elder Scaevola, often called the "Augur," was the most learned figure of his age and used his ability in litigation to demonstrate the "justice" of his causes.[54] As a character in *De Oratore*, Scaevola disapproved of schematic rhetoric as much as Crassus and Antonius disliked technical jurisprudence. In addition to the Elder Scaevola's command of legal science and rhetorically "uncontaminated" litigation, Cicero praised his ability to incorporate ethical principles of Stoicism into a legal concept of *bona fides*.[55]

The traits of the Elder Scaevola, which earned Cicero's praise, were even more clearly demonstrated in the Younger Scaevola, often called the "Pontifex." Cicero held great regard for Scaevola, considering him one of the most competent orators among the jurists.[56] Perhaps even more of a legal scholar than the Augur, Scaevola published one of the first known systematic treatises on the civil law, *Ius Civile*, which was the foundation for many later commentaries. Like the Augur, the Younger Scaevola incorporated his ethical principles into his deliberative and forensic rhetoric. Cicero once mocked Verres as a "Scaevola" since the Younger Scaevola's reputation as a fair governor made the name a synonym for equity.[57] Although Cicero considered Crassus more prudent than Scaevola, his comments on the confrontation of the two advocates in the famous *Causa Curiana* indicate that Scaevola's strict interpretation of the wording of a will was a worthy challenge to Crassus' urbanity.[58] Cicero summarized his praise of the Younger Scaevola in the *De Oratore* through Crassus: "the most educated man in the study of civil law, the most acute in natural ability and practical judgment . . . the most eloquent of expert advocates and the most expert of eloquent advocates."[59]

Servius Sulpicius Rufus also possessed many qualities of effective jurisprudence which Cicero admired. A close personal friend, Sulpicius studied rhetoric with Cicero in Rome and went with him to Rhodes for additional instruction.[60] No speeches of Sulpicius are extant, possibly because Sulpicius loathed writing, but his style was so lofty that Cicero thought of him as a tragic actor in the courtroom.[61] Cicero's attitude toward Sulpicius' oratorical style is important, especially when compared with the Younger Scaevola, who was known for his brevity.[62] Cicero regarded both as experts in legal science, but their styles were quite different. Therefore, we can conclude that Cicero connected no single speaking style with being a "technician" of forensic rhetoric. Servius Sulpicius mastered and employed dialectic.[63] The Younger Scaevola limited himself to a simplistic style and apparently applied no philosophical principles of inquiry beyond the ethical precepts of Stoicism. Sulpicius, however, was regarded more highly than the Younger Scaevola not for any one level of eloquence (plain, middle, or grand), but for his mastery of dialectic.[64]

Although Cicero decried ability in legal science in the *Pro Murena*, he demonstrated his knowledge of jurisprudence in such cases as the *Pro Caecina*. Crassus and Antonius, as characters in *De Oratore*, lampooned advocates who stressed legal science, but an examination of Cicero's personal attitude and practice reveals a strong admiration for the legal talents of such orators and jurists as the Scaevolae and Sulpicius. Cicero praised the Scaevolae for their ability to analyze and interpret fine legal points and for uniting Stoic morality with legal principles of equity. Cicero admired Sulpicius, however, as the best of all "technicians" of forensic rhetoric and jurists because he united a thorough knowledge of law with dialectic and polished his oratorical style to such a high degree that a blend of *eloquentia* and *doctrina* resulted.

In essence, Cicero believed that a knowledge of legal science and dialectic and high moral standards were desirable but should be made subtly apparent to listeners—probably because such traits hold less appeal than the histrionics of forensic rhetors such as Marcus Antonius. Ideally, the orator avoids a technical appearance by embellishing fine legal points with an active, entertaining style that pleases the listener. While some of Cicero's speeches argue legal issues, they elevate the argument to higher levels than the fine points of jurisprudence. It would be a good guess that Cicero did have many tedious trials, yet his extant written compositions tend to transcend petty debates and stress more captivating social issues. While no evidence could be reconstructed to support such a claim, it is likely that Cicero's published orations allowed him to introduce dramatic clashes that may never have been so lively in court. Sensitivity to the desires of audiences is a trait no one questions in Cicero, and his orations may have been occasions to edit for dramatic vitality rather than technical accuracy.

Uncompromising Culture Heroes of Stoic Rhetoric: Cato the Censor and Cato Uticensis, the Marci Porcii Catones

Two Romans named Marcus Porcius Cato distinguished themselves in Roman history and earned the praise of Cicero as accomplished advocates. Marcus Porcius Cato the Censor (234–149 B.C.) preceded Cicero by approximately two generations. Cicero praised the Elder Cato for his perspicuity and studied over one hundred and fifty of his speeches, commending them for their argumentation and diction.[65] Cato's particular strength as a speaker was his ability to unite a thorough knowledge of civil law with strong ethical principles.[66] Cato first popularized the concept of "the good man speaking well" (*vir bonus dicendi peritus*), which influenced Cicero's *vir bonus* concept and inspired Quintilian's *Institutio oratoria*.[67]

Several rhetorical traits of Marcus Porcius Cato Uticensis, the great-grandson of the Elder Cato, were both praised and criticized by Cicero. When Cicero defended Murena, he praised the *ingenium* of Cato, who was one of the opposing advocates, calling him "the foundation and rigor of the whole prosecution."[68] Cato's major strengths were his uncompromising morality and tenacious commitment to a cause.[69] Cicero noted Cato's speaking style as brief and claimed that he demonstrated a certain enthusiasm and personal influence or *auctoritas*.[70] Cicero's main criticism of Cato, however, was his narrow, Stoic-style oratory. In essence, Cicero praised the morality of Stoicism but criticized other precepts which Stoics such as Cato presented in their causes.[71] Such Stoic beliefs as the claim that all crimes were equally bad were lampooned by Cicero throughout the *Pro Murena*.[72] Cicero also believed that the logic of the Stoics was no actual progression in dialectic, and that their sobriety deterred compassion—which must have been all too apparent to listeners.[73] Cato Uticensis, like his renowned great-grandfather, was highly regarded as a shrewd and moralistic advocate. Yet strict adherence to Stoic principles inhibited pragmatism and conciliation—essential qualities for daily life in the courts of the Roman Republic.

Despite Cicero's taunts at Cato in the *Pro Murena*, he recognized personal authority as a potent force in legal argument. Cato and his family had the luxury of a long tradition of service and uncompromising virtue. Prior credibility, as Aristotle indicates, is only one form of *ethos*, for individuals can gain credibility within an oration. Certainly for Cicero, who did not possess a patrician lineage, establishing his credibility by legal arguments not only aided in gaining immediate decisions but in securing a public image after the written orations were publicly available.

Conclusion

An analysis of the traits of Cicero's rhetorical ancestors reveals five points of significance in understanding Cicero's forensic rhetoric and the nature of the courts. First, Cicero recognized no single formula for success, no one particular rhetorical style that was most effective. In fact, the notion of seeking the perfect advocate would only blind the inquirer to the many sources of success and inspiration which Cicero recognized and from which he drew.

Second, the standards by which Cicero criticized advocates were drawn primarily from popular judgment. Cicero may have had more personal respect or dislike for a particular advocate than the public, but he never contradicted public opinion completely. The reason for Cicero's consistency with the populace was that his criteria were fundamentally audience-centered and audience-derived. Cicero may have isolated and explained the particular qualities which made an advocate successful, but it is imperative to realize that his praise and analysis was *ex post facto*; it was predicated on an advocate already establishing himself with the people or jurors.

Third, because success was audience-dependent, it was important that an advocate present an appearance and style favored by listeners. Occasionally, an advocate faced a conflict wherein the jurors looked for technical arguments and the populace for emotive appeals and histrionics. In this situation, the effectiveness of the speaker—in light of the inferences drawn from this study—was measured by his ability to secure the favor of as many parts of the audience as possible.

Fourth, in addition to the favor of the audience, certain fundamental traits were discovered which Cicero admired in the advocates he praised. These traits can be classified into six areas: the ability to employ the technical precepts of rhetoric, including the canon of memory; natural talent; the presentation of a positive and forceful image; zeal and industry; proficiency in reasoning; and an awareness and application of ethics. These can be justly inferred as traits Cicero associated with successful advocates and included in a standard for his own forensic rhetoric. Subsequent chapters will examine Cicero's forensic rhetoric in light of these characteristics.

Fifth, the relationship of writing to oral argument is evident in two instrumental functions: as an aid to memory in the composition of oral arguments and as means of preserving texts of speeches for pedagogy and posterity. Writing was used in the formulation of oral arguments when compositions were written out and memorized for presentation while transcriptions of legal arguments served a heuristic function as models for study. Certainly, Cicero benefited from these traditional uses of writing. But Cicero extended the uses of writing to facilitate modes of conceptualizing discourse and—in the posttrial publication of texts—wrote documents which were presented as speeches but were actually eloquently written literary statements. Empowered by a degree of literacy superior to any earlier or contemporary Roman, and sensitive to the need for capturing oral characteristics in written legal compositions, Cicero sought to persuade listeners at the trial and to animate the posttrial publication. While these later compositons may not have matched the actual events, they employed techniques that would, in the words of Father Walter J. Ong, give the written composition a "heavy oral residue."[74]

3

The Epistemological Foundation

A history of literature is not concerned with politics or even morality except insofar as they affect readibility.
L. P. Wilkinson, The Cambridge History of Classical Literature

In his work *Orality and Literacy: The Technologizing of the Word*, Walter J. Ong credits Cicero's "deadly targeting on issues and on adversaries' weaknesses" as "the work of a literate mind." In the same passage Father Ong claims that "Cicero did not compose his orations in script before he gave them but wrote down afterwards the texts that we now have." [1] Father Ong's point is certainly an important one for his thesis, since Cicero did have extensive preparation and practice in written composition and evidently used his skill in his forensic rhetoric. One of Ong's chief sources for claiming that Cicero did not compose his orations beforehand is the meticulous and comprehensive work of Torsten Petersson, *Cicero: A Biography*. A review of the relevant passages of Petersson's work, however, offers a view different from Ong's. Petersson asserts that Cicero was "always an ardent believer in writing as an aid to speaking" and "seems to have composed and memorized any passages that he would be likely to use."[2] From his analysis of primary and secondary sources, Petersson claims that "as a result, much of a speech even in court, and still more in the forum and the senate, was composed beforehand; and Cicero could use all this in the published oration."[3]

Our goal, then, is to reconcile theories of Cicero's literacy in legal argument. There is little doubt that Petersson is accurate in his view that Cicero used writing as an aid to speaking. Father Ong's comments, however, need to be qualified for their merits to be understood and appreciated fully. Father Ong addresses the published versions of Cicero's speeches, that is, the documents presented as "speeches" after the trial. In this sense, these publicly distributed texts were neither written (as such) before the trial nor delivered verbatim; in this regard, Father Ong is accurate. Yet to leave the discussion at this level is to neglect the rich relationship writing and speaking had for Cicero in legal argument. Cicero's literate mind doubtlessly helped him to compose and memorize a speech before a trial as Petersson claims. Similarly, Cicero's literate mind aided in the composition of a written text of a "speech" for publication, as Ong rightly observes. There is, however, another dimension to Cicero's literate mind that transcends the reproduction and transmission of oral argument: the conceptual processes that writing facilitates. Writing freezes words and makes abstract, analytical thought more accessible. Similarly, stabilizing concepts permits one to ponder highly defined, hypotactic structures and modalities of expression more readily. Along with his study of rhetoric, Cicero's training in philosophy exposed him to these conceptual patterns and syntactic structures. More importantly, and in reconciliation of the views of Petersson and Ong, combining his study of rhetoric and philosophy permitted him to apply such modes of thought through a technology (writing) that fostered abstract thinking. Such skills would, in turn, be beneficial both in the written preparation of a trial speech and in the posttrial publication. Thus, to appreciate Cicero's literate mind in legal rhetoric we must also recognize how his philosophical training enhanced his oral and written expression.

Cicero was not the first Roman to benefit from philosophy, but the merits of this Greek contribution were treated with reservation by many traditional Romans. Although Romans of the late Republic are commonly cast as willing beneficiaries of Greek culture, their initial reaction toward the disciplines of rhetoric and philosophy demonstrated little philhellenism. In a culture where a subject was evaluated by its utility, the disdain for both Hellenic disciplines became quite strong.[4] Despite initial objections, however, Romans eventually assimilated rhetoric, in part because of its utility in the courts and government. Yet to pragmatic Roman minds, philosophy, without apparent practical application, was barely endured.[5] Nevertheless, the benefits of a cooperative study of both disciplines were apparent to Cicero, who recognized their value to argument and expression.

Cicero's decided advantage as an advocate was his literate mind. Earlier chapters revealed the importance of writing in Cicero's education. Comments on his earliest education show a strong and steady interest in writing. His advanced education, particularly in Greece, underscores the stress on rhetorical composition so essential to logography. His prolific capacity as a letter-writer, his numerous treatises on rhetoric and philosophy, and the frequent publication of his deliberative and forensic orations add dimensions to our already secure knowledge that Cicero was a man of letters in a culture dominated by orality. Yet facile expression does not alone make for the literate mentality being discussed here. Cicero recognized that areas other than rhetoric indirectly develop proficiency in expression, that eloquence is the result of an informed, analytical mind. While even a casual reading of *De Oratore* makes this point obvious, what is not so readily apparent is his use of writing in shaping thought for oral presentation. Training in philosophy stressed reasoning processes and modes of expression which could be valuable in the courts but were not conventional to oral argument as it was practiced. While writing does not control philosophical thought, it is clear that writing's capacity to "freeze" notions can facilitate modes of thought and expression. Specifically, considering abstract concepts, articulating apodictic and coexistent relationships, and structuring prose-rhythmic passages that articulate such relationships lucidly benefit from writing ability. We know that writing was considered essential to legal argument. But Cicero used writing not only as an aid in memorizing oral argument but as a medium which prompted complex modes of thought and expression reflecting sophistication not apparent in previous advocates. The correlations between philosophical thought and rhetorical expression cannot be too heavily stressed if we hope to understand Cicero's unique position as an advocate. His contributions as a rhetorical theorist have been well recognized, and scholars such as Alain Michel have indicated how his rhetorical and philosophical views relate to his theoretical concept of law.[6] No major works, however, have examined two aspects of philosophy that relate to his forensic rhetoric: dialectic and ethics.

Philosophy, Rhetoric, and Legal Argument

Cicero believed that there was a natural unity between philosophy and rhetoric, a unity which facilitated a fuller understanding of the nature of man.[7] The link between the disciplines of rhetoric and philosophy was the search for truth through reason, a bond which necessitated an understanding of the basic principles of rhetoric.[8] Cicero believed that reason helped to make virtue logically apparent.[9] Thus an advocate ought to employ philosophical inquiry with rhetorical strategies in a judgmental process for the realization of probable truth and its complement, justice. Ciceronian litigation centered on the notion that the natural intelligence of man provided the rational basis for justice. Ignorance, or lack of natural intelligence, necessitated litigation.[10] Since philosophy and rhetoric both sought truth, and the goal of litigation was to facilitate the highest level of understanding, the reinstatement of justice required the forensic rhetor to make truth apparent through the aid of philosophy and rhetoric.[11] But rhetoric and philosophy had been kept mutually exclusive since Plato: philosophers were trained in understanding and orators in expression.[12] Consequently, the rift between rhetoric and philosophy had separated not only dialectic from oratory, but also eloquence from philosophy.

Cicero maintained that philosophy was important to rhetoric because of its concern with method and to forensic rhetoric in particular because of its power to influence decisions.[13] This belief was particularly evident in his philosophical allegiance to the New Academy. "For the orator holds a strong association with this kind of philosophy which I follow," wrote Cicero, "since he borrows exactness from the Academy and repays the debt with a rich oratory and an embellished style."[14] Cicero felt that an advocate who effectively united principles of philosophy with rhetoric would have the persuasive ability to convince his jurors as philosophers did their listeners; in short, he believed that "a complete orator possesses all the knowledge of philosophers, yet eloquence is not necessarily in the learning of philosophers; which, however, as much as it is despised by philosophers, is nevertheless considered necessary in order to set some sort of crown upon their theories."[15] Knowing that Cicero realized the advantages of applying philosophy with rhetoric is of little value unless the specific advantages which philosophy held for forensic rhetoric can be isolated and examined. This understanding can be accomplished by observing Cicero's thoughts on those Roman advocates who did unite them.

Ethics, Dialectics, and the "Reasonable"

Cicero believed that Quintus Mucius Scaevola was one of the most learned legal figures of the preceding generation.[16] In addition to a thorough knowledge of litigation, the Elder Scaevola had the ability to incorporate strong ethical principles of Stoicism into a legal concept of equity.[17] These traits were also evident in the Younger Quintus Mucius Scaevola. Cicero's attitude toward the two Scaevolae reveals a point of major significance: effective jurisprudence entails an ability to construct rhetorical strategies which are predicated on acceptable ethical presumptions. But arguments not only must demonstrate ethical standards but also a proper form of presentation. For this structure of argumentation Cicero again drew on the disciplines of rhetoric and philosophy.

Cicero's respect for his colleague, Servius Sulpicius Rufus, reveals his understanding that rhetorical strategies and the manifestation of laudable values were not definitive characteristics of successful litigation.[18] They required an argumentative form that would be acceptable to the Republican courts. In essence, a methodology for presentation was required which could transform philosophical presuppositions into pragmatic wranglings. Cicero identified this ability in Sulpicius: "I think, Brutus, that Scaevola and many others had a great use of civil law: in Sulpicius it was an art, which he never would have accomplished with jurisprudence itself, except that in addition he learned an art which taught how to divide a whole thing into its parts, to uncover the hidden by defining, to explain the obscure by interpreting, first to see ambiguities, then to distinguish, finally to have a rule by which truths and falsehood could be judged and which things were first premises and which were consequences."[19] Cicero's comment introduces the second point of significance in isolating specific aspects of philosophy in litigation: Sulpicus mastered a philosophical process imperative to forensic argumentation—dialectic. Where the Scaevolae stressed perspicuity and emphasized ethical principles of Stoicism, Sulpicius utilized the philosophical procedure of dialectic to demonstrate and perfect his forensic rhetoric. Thus, an advocate could readily employ his knowledge of rhetoric and philosophy to develop a clear and defensible ethical basis for arguments and adapt dialectic as a critical courtroom tool. In brief, principles of dialectic and ethics constitute the philosophical foundation for Cicero's litigation strategies. The remaining task then is to examine the specific nature and role of Ciceronian "dialectic" and "ethics" in the courts of the Roman Republic.

Cicero's major philosophical positions, particularly in the area of dialectic, came from the Academy.[20] Virtually ignoring the doctrines of the Old Academy, Cicero nevertheless held its leading figure, Plato, in high esteem—especially for the notion of seeking truth without deception.[21] Despite a qualified praise for Plato's eloquence, Cicero strongly criticized Socrates, who—although not a member of the Old Academy—personified in the "Gorgias" the Platonic concept of separating eloquence from philosophy.[22] The problem with this seperation was the absence of the logical analysis characteristic of philosophy, which Cicero considered critical to the rigorous argumentation of forensic rhetors.[23]

Cicero adopted a modified approach for forensic rhetoric developed from the epistemological maxim of the Middle Academy, Scepticism. Traditionally, Scepticism advocated suspended judgment, the avoidance of a positive thesis, an emphasis in refutation, and a moral commitment to the "reasonable." Cicero's belief in the existence of truth, his disavowal of Sceptic inaction because of disapproval, and his condemnation of Sceptic aloofness from ethical issues prompted him to reject several of their extreme positions.[24] Yet his interpretation and defense of select Sceptic tenets reveals his convictions on the nature of litigation and the necessity of conjoining the dialectical process of philosophy with rhetoric in forensics.[25] Cicero maintained throughout the second book of *Academica* that man acquired beliefs that are assimilated into attitudes through his senses. This position led Cicero to argue that certainty could not be attained through the senses, not only because of man's inherent limitations but also because it is impossible to discern truth from falsehood. Cicero's admission to the imperceptibility of truth isolated him from such dogmatic ethical philosophies as Stoicism and Platonism, which claimed dialectical systems of inquiry that led to certain knowledge and virtue. These philosophies, which argued that truth was independent of the senses and that logic framed in a dialectical manner led to absolute knowledge, necessitated absolute conclusions.

Cicero took strong exception to such philosophical schools, particularly when their positions of absolutism were applied to litigation. Since certainty was beyond the perception of man, Cicero believed that carefully constructed arguments based on probability ought to serve as a guide for the judgment of human conduct. Such an epistemology posited that while truth was imperceptible it was not nonexistent. Consequently, if dialectic could be adapted from the quest for logical certainty and used to attain probable judgments, then a closer approximation to truth could be advanced. Furthermore, eloquence which could direct and clarify perception would serve to aid the dialectical process in the attainment of this goal. In short, Cicero believed it was foolish to assent to allegedly certain conclusions, which some philosophical schools claimed to attain; he thought it more reasonable to hold an opinion with the qualification that it was probable and subject to reexamination.[26] His interpretation of Scepticism fostered a strong emphasis in probability, an emphasis appropriate to the inferential judgment required in legal proceedings.[27]

The dialectic of the New Academy necessitated examination and counterexamination through a discussion of both sides of a dispute. Cicero adhered to the Academic practice of dialectical inquiry "because it was not possible in any other way for a probable point to be discovered in each case, but also because it was an especially good exercise in speaking."[28] Cicero believed the Old Academy's major flaw was that their philosophers insufficiently prepared students for the law courts. "Accordingly," he wrote, "forensic eloquence was rejected and scorned by many philosophers and actually lost a great deal of support; but yet, embellished with expressions and epigrams, it kept striving after popularity and was not afraid of the opinion and censure of the few. Consequently, the educated were lacking refined learning."[29] In essence, Cicero shifted the dialectic focal point from the perception of certainty to the rhetorical quest for probability, a system—Cicero argued—which was well suited to the argumentative structure of the courts because it recognized the uncertainty of perception and the risk of inference.[30]

For Cicero, the dialectical method of the New Academy helped to bridge the gap between philosophy and forensic rhetoric. The critical method of the New Academy functioned in a situation where judgment rested with both jurors and populace, for this epistemological position discouraged the establishment of definitive conclusions and encouraged judgment grounded in probability and established through the revelation of the listener. Reluctance to advance definitive conclusions was vital to the very judicial process, where the resolution of a decision rested on the contingent perception of the jurors and listeners, and not on the axiomatically based tautologies of a pleader. The nature of this approach required advocates to set forth rhetorically their philosophical rationale to groups of unsophisticated listeners.

The significance of Ciceronian dialectic is further apparent when examining its relationship to his ethical standards. Cicero considered justice inherent in the supreme law of reason and thus capable of being intuitively recognized.[31] The task of a forensic orator was to employ dialectic in the preparation and perhaps in the presentation of his case in order to demonstrate the reasonableness and justice of his cause to his listeners.

Arguing at Romans

Since listeners formulated beliefs that resulted in decisions, the most powerful force an advocate could possess was an ability to direct the attitudes of his listeners, since "the very quality of a distinguished orator is that he is recognized as a distinguished orator by the populace."[32] Although successful advocates often stressed plausibility and well-structured orations, they were primarily students of human nature, histrionics, and audience analysis. "Now nothing in speaking," wrote Cicero, "is as important for an orator as securing the favor of his listener, and to have the listener so aroused that he is guided by a sort of mental impulse and emotion as well as by judgment and deliberation."[33] Lines of argument were reinforced with emotive appeals which were directed toward eliciting responses of approval and disapproval. These appeals would, in turn, aid in shaping attitudes that would influence the acceptance of new beliefs. While such views were probably shared by many of his colleagues, Cicero's ability to apply the systematic training he received in philosophy would likely make his methods of reasoning more refined then those orators who relied on their own suppositions and individual methods.

The Roman courts were the natural arena for probable argument. As Cicero maintained, "the activity of the orator consists of opinions, not knowledge" because orators "speak to those who are ignorant and we [orators] speak on things we ourselves do not know."[34] Cicero believed strongly that jurors ought to be versed in argumentation, but his concern was not with their ability to understand and interpret points of law.[35] Cicero theorized that the forensic rhetor should be particularly sensitive to the attitudes, thoughts, and beliefs of the jurors in order to arouse responses to the fundamental justice of the issue.[36] In essence, whether the listeners were the unsophisticated crowd that frequently flocked to important trials or the *nobiles* who presided as jurors, the forensic rhetor sought to secure the conviction of his audience by clarifying the ethical principles upon which his cause was founded.[37]

Forensic argument was based on the condition that validity is determined by the audience. That is, the listeners, not an artificially contrived system of formal proofs, determine what is convincing. Since adherence of interlocutors was the driving force, it is no wonder that Cicero was guided by probability, where lines of argument rested upon the credibility of inferences and decisions secured by assent.[38] These conditions reveal the rationale for the dialectical method which Cicero advanced. The *status*, or point of dispute in a case, formed the focal point of counterarguments; such a procedure enabled the listeners to evaluate the case in accordance with their values. Consequently, the dialectical "revelation" was actually the acquiescence of a cause in the form of a verdict established upon the credence of probability demonstrated by a line of argument. A successful advocate united the compressed argumentation of dialectic with rhetorical embellishment for the purpose of stimulating a line of argumentation.[39]

Realizing the values that were operative in a case was not only imperative for proficiency in dialectic but also explains Cicero's concern for the study of ethics. Adhering to his eclectic position, Cicero incorporated Sceptic and New Academy concepts of probability and dialectic with Stoic tenets of morality. While Cicero disagreed with much of Stoic philosophy and severely criticized its irrelevance and laconic style, he nonetheless admired the Stoic emphasis in dialectic and deductive reasoning.[40] His main affiliation with Stoicism, however, centered upon certain ethical concepts. Rejecting the dogmatism of Stoic principles, Cicero's moral philosophy for litigation was an adaptation of Zeno's observation that moral worth was the only good.[41] Cicero modified ethical tenets of Stoicism into a morality for courtroom pleading, for he constantly stressed the inherent value of moral worth: "nothing ought to be desired for its own sake, except that which is morally good."[42]

Cicero's perplexingly vague interpretations of virtue may have intentionally avoided a prescriptive moral code for the courts. Yet the process by which Ciceronian morality functioned in litigation is evident. Cicero believed that since "virtue is reason developed . . . so also is everything morally good in the natural order of things."[43] H. A. K. Hunt argued that Cicero believed morality was attained through a development of virtues, which implies that if Cicero maintained that virtue was developed through reason, then his ethical position would become apparent to listeners as his argument developed.[44] The point of significance, however, is that this morality was not only the most probable approach but also the most credible principle of justification. The circumstances of a particular case never justified suspending moral obligations for the sake of an expedient position. Thus, an expedient position, if it is to satisfy the necessary conditions of a virtuous act, must not only be morally justified but must also be readily apparent to listeners.

An example of this process of ethical revelation occurred in Cicero's prosecution of Gaius Verres. Throughout the case Cicero attempted to appeal to the attitudes of his listeners by conveying the impression that his argument was predicated on moral issues. He sought to portray the prosecution as arguing from a highly ethical standpoint while presenting the defense as a mockery to Roman morality, to convince the audience that the prosecution of Verres was actually a defense of Roman values. Through an awesome presentation of factual evidence, testimony, and reasoning he was able to reveal Verres' immorality while indirectly establishing his own honorable position. His ability to illustrate the moral discrepancy between two sides is evident in the *Divinatio*, *Actio Prima*, and Book I of the *Actio Secunda*, where he argued that he represented the Sicilians, that he was a Roman providing a public service to the Republic. "I am defending many men, many cities, and the entire province of Sicily. Therefore, because I believe this one man ought to be prosecuted, I seem, in a way, to continue my custom and not entirely to depart from defending and supporting individuals."[45]

Quintilian echoed Cicero in declaring that a good man preferred defense but must take up the prosecution when the welfare of the Republic was threatened.[46] Cicero established himself as a champion of Roman values, a *vir bonus* whose motive was to check Verres' corruption for the defense of the State. Such ethical standards enabled him to present his prosecution as a reinstatement of traditional Roman values, continually reminding the Senatorial Order that guarding allies' rights upheld the traditions of such forefathers as Marcus Cato Sapiens and Gnaeus Domitius.[47] These tactics were quite typical and illustrate a clear advantage for uniting rhetoric and the ethical standards of Stoic philosophy in forensic discourse.

Cicero's capacity to articulate his dialectical abilities and ethical positions as a defense advocate is also attested in his forensic rhetoric. An examination of his *Pro Quinctio*, *Pro Roscio Amerino*, and *Pro Caecina* exemplify his capacity in dialectic. Moreover, his ability to isolate the moral issues of a case are evident in *Pro Rabirio Perduellionis* and *Pro Murena*. On occasion, Cicero would forsake either his dialectical procedure or his avowed ethical position in order to secure the decision of a particular case. These departures are apparent, but equally recognizable is Cicero's capacity to marry rhetoric and philosophy with dialectic and a familiarity with ethics. Such orations reveal the training in philosophy that provided the sophistication to elevate his arguments beyond convention.

Cicero indicates that knowledge of dialectic and ethics were not ancillary benefits to an advocate but rather qualifications for excellence since the speech act was itself a dialectical structure culminating in a synthesis of values. The end of philosophy, as in litigation, is the revelation of truth. The prosecution and defense were each representatives of the juxtaposition which provided *pro* and *contra* theses. Propositions advanced were, consequently, not analytic but synthetic since judgment was determined not through logic but metaphysics. That is, the method by which judgments were secured rested not within the self-containment of a tautological concept but rather to an outside standard of unprovable premises: the values of the listeners who rendered a judgment. The judgment of advocates was therefore suspended and the decision rested with the opinion of the jurors and ultimately the public at large; that is, the values upon which they believed truth or justice to be predicated. Since the rhetorical act was not a self-contained analytic process, it necessarily rested outside the realm of certainty and in the province of probability. Such an explanation clarifies how this dialectical process was predicated upon probability since the principle of justification is inherently within the metaphysical presuppositions of ethics, particularly the first principles of justice and equity.

Summary and Conclusion

This chapter illustrates three areas of reconciliation between rhetoric and philosophy that were important to Cicero's forensic rhetoric. First, an understanding of philosophy was valuable to an advocate since the unity of rhetoric and philosophy aided in the discovery of probable truth. Second, Cicero believed that an advocate should withhold assent, assess antithetical positions, and demonstrate an ability to employ principles of argumentation so thoroughly that he could master the uses of probability and dialectic. Third, Cicero thought an advocate should be virtuous and direct his arguments toward the chief good. In fact, he believed that moral worth was desirable in an advocate and in the courts for its own sake and was recognizable through reason. Philosophy, joined with his established proficiency in writing, enabled Cicero to produce sophisticated arguments with rigor directed toward securing the favor of his audiences.

Cicero united dialectic and ethics to advocacy through his belief that virtue was grounded in man's natural reason. Thus, employment of probability—a tool of argumentation—was used to uncover the reasonableness of a cause and ultimately justice. As the critical process of dialectic was developed, the virtue of a cause also became apparent since the superior moral worth of an advocate's case produced a favorable attitude grounded in reason. The unification of rhetoric and philosophy aided in discovering and making apparent probable truth in accordance with the values of jurors and listeners. Through these disciplines, advocates developed proficiency in counter-argumentation and gained insight into probability and dialectic. Most important of all, an advocate could advance logical arguments in provocative discourse based on "virtuous" premises for pragmatic Roman listeners. The confluence of these skills within legal argument helped to develop a literate mind which approached advocacy in a manner not previously seen in the courts of the Republic.

To say that Cicero used writing for his legal rhetoric is to advance a statement rich in dimensions. Cicero used writing as an aid to memory in the preparation of his cases. He also used writing for posttrial publication of his speeches. This chapter has shown a third dimension in the relationship of Cicero's orality and literacy. Cicero marshaled his knowledge and skills of philosophy to enrich his forensic rhetoric. His ability in writing provided a technology that enabled him to isolate and freeze concepts more easily than if he relied on verbal expression alone. Thus the depth of his arguments both in the oral and published versions would be enhanced by his philosophical skill. Yet the benefits of philosophy became apparent in his legal rhetoric because his literate prowess more easily induced abstract thought and held it for the sort of oratorical and (eventually) literary polish that earned Cicero enduring fame.

4

The Audiences of Cicero's Rhetoric

Cicero writes academic rhetorical theory, but when he pleads he utilizes every opportunity to win his case.
George Kennedy, The Art of Rhetoric in the Roman World

Because of our preoccupation with "the text" there exists an inclination to examine orations of the Republic independent of the climate that prompted their initial composition, to neglect the audience as a factor in the rhetorical events, to concentrate on literary features exclusive of contextual factors. The success of Roman advocates depended on their popularity with listeners who daily filled the Forum to appreciate and evaluate rhetorical skill. Yet long after Cicero's forensic orations lost their relevancy to immediate issues they endured as lively models of argument. Understanding why distanced audiences can appreciate Cicero's speeches as well as his immediate audiences did reveals his mastery at preserving the dynamic features of orality in his writing. At the heart of this relationship is his sensitivity to different audiences, the importance of transcending the immediate situation, and using the orations as a means of composing a favorable public image. Audience approval was an influencing factor to advocates such as Cicero; it prompted them to convey a popular image in order to gain recognition. In fact, Roman orators often concentrated less on values and more on conveying a favorable image.

Sustaining popularity after the cheers of the trial, however, was facilitated by published speeches which not only recorded proceedings but captured the dynamism of the event. The published, posttrial oration served, in turn, to create a *persona* for the posttrial audience, which was encouraged to recognize the merits of the advocate as a "good man" (*vir bonus*) in the service of Rome.

The Rhetorical Climate

The primary site for oratory—whether deliberative, forensic, or epideictic—was the Forum.[1] As a center of Roman civic activity, the Forum frequently held such large crowds that speakers had to shout their orations in order to be audible.[2] Amid this dense and incessant stream of human traffic the Rostra functioned as the topographical focal point in oratory.[3] As Roman litigation developed into an established institution, conviction was secured increasingly by colorful oratory—particularly in cases of a violent or personal nature. Similarly, Senate members frequently interrupted proceedings with boisterous cries of approval and disapproval.[4] Such overt responses provided a climate which cultivated pathetic oratory and prompted considerable attention to capturing and impressing listeners. The combined factors of the Roman ego, growing common audiences, and the orator's attention to stylistics created—over a period of time—a popular attraction for citizens and a flattering platform for speakers. Hired applauders accented a pleader's cause and the din of the orator and his supporters often provided an entertaining, almost circus-like arena. Jerome Carcopino captured the spirit of this atmosphere claiming "that the thunder of one of the defending counsels filled the vast hall and drowned the controversies in the other chambers. In one notorious instance Galerius Tracalus . . . whose voice was extraordinarily powerful, was greeted with the public applause of all four chambers, three of which could not see him and ought not to have heard him."[5] The effects were evident on the crowd and on the orator, both of whom became consumed by their involvement.[6] In a time of moral decay and political crisis, the Rostra became the platform for the articulation of Roman values, sometimes well beyond the point at issue. Trials were flavored with scandal, heightened by legal eloquence, and fueled by listeners who, Carcopino adds, were held "immobile and spellbound hour after hour in the neighbourhood of the tribunals."[7] The audience was a force no advocate could afford to dismiss. Despite their obvious presence, the nature and composition of the Roman listeners in the Late Republic is virtually unknown. The Roman "audience," therefore, must be discussed if we are to understand the notions of immediate and distanced audiences in Ciceronian Rome.

The Immediate Audience in Ciceronian Rome

The popular audience of the Late Republic became a dominant social force as political power began to shift from the patrician to the lesser equestrian and plebeian classes. Such a perspective is clearly evident to Cicero, who believed that the goal of eloquence was to gain the approval of listeners and insisted that "the very quality of a distinguished orator is that he is recognized as a distinguished orator by the populace."[8] It is no wonder, then, why Cicero believed that the more adept an orator became, the more he should concern himself with audience analysis.[9] Cicero's remarks reveal his preoccupation with producing a favorable attitude in the listener's mind: "the controller of oratory has always been the discretion of the listeners. For all who wish to be approved respect the wants of those who listen, and entirely shape and adapt themselves to that [end], to their judgment and will."[10]

Having the audience set the standard for successful rhetoric had profound implications for composing arguments. The tumultuous climate for oral arguments encouraged approval based predominantly on emotive responses. In order to secure a favorable audience opinion, an advocate needed to discern the attitudes of his listeners and adapt his position "to the time, the nature of the controversy, and person."[11] He asserted that everyone would "admit that out of all the merits of an orator by far the greatest is to arouse the spirits of the listeners and to bend them whatever way the situation should demand; he who lacks this quality is missing that which is the greatest merit."[12] Cicero, not surprisingly, believed that while a speaker may have been recognized as wise, he would never have been considered eloquent and received shouts of acclaim and applause unless he appealed to the senses of his listeners.[13] Composing an oral argument to such an audience prompted the use of emotive appeals and other extralogical techniques. Such techniques were both standard and expected in the wranglings of the Roman courts of the Republic. To read these forensic orations without this presupposition, however, makes the speeches easy prey for critics who would fault Cicero and his fellow advocates for imprecise thinking or unethical tactics. Adjusting for the context involves realizing that Cicero was speaking before listeners whose expectations were diverse and whose presumptions for conventional techniques were far different from our own. Understanding such refinements in audience is important not only to appreciate how speeches were composed for the immediate audience but how they were adapted eventually to the distanced audiences who later read them as models of eloquence.

Distinguishing Groups of Listeners

Advocates such as Cicero were compelled to consider two distinct groups of listeners. The first group was made up of the masses, those listeners who daily filled the Forum; the second group was composed of jurists and civic leaders, high-ranking citizens who evaluated the cases and rendered decisions. Traditionally, the upper classes of Roman society had received almost exclusively the attention of the orators, but within a few generations of the career of Cicero, the importance of popular audiences to oratory became apparent. Lucius Licinius Crassus was the first orator to initiate the practice of speaking away from the *nobiles* and toward the general public gathered in the Forum.[14] Although Tacitus maintained that the common crowd was unsophisticated, orators such as Antonius believed that oratory should be adapted to the ears of the general populace.[15]

By Cicero's time, huge crowds were common at important trials, and remarks such as we find in the *In Verrem* and *Pro Sestio* indicate that Cicero was accustomed to speaking before large audiences.[16] Many forensic rhetors had "supporters" or *advocationes* among the crowds to shout biased praises for their orator.[17] Yet accurate audience analysis was extremely difficult for an advocate in almost any speaking situation. As a letter from Cicero to Atticus attests: "I wrote to you earlier about what Pompey's first public speech was like, the poor were not pleased, the rebellious considered it worthless, the rich were ungrateful, the conservatives thought it unimportant, so it fell flat."[18]

For any speaker, misinterpreted or unanticipated audience reaction easily could lead to disaster. There were certain signs, however, which Roman advocates recognized in attempting to measure the reaction of an audience. The most obvious cue was applause. While there is no substantial evidence to indicate that jurists also applauded to indicate approval, the popular audiences showed little reluctance to express their emotions. Throughout his works, Cicero notes public admiration in the form of applause and "shouts of approval"; for instance, after his *Pro Milone* Cicero commented that "the applause which was given to him [Milo] seemed in a way to be given to me."[19] As with many orators of his time, Brutus became so dependent upon the responses of a popular audience, that he felt he was unable to speak to a bench of judges unless he was surrounded also by a circle of active listeners.[20]

In certain instances an orator could actually control the composition of his audience. Such a situation is evident in litigation, where knowledge of the jury members was especially important, particularly because the prosecutor often was given the discretion of jury selection by the *Lex Plautia de Vi.*[21] Thus, since selection of jurors often became selection of part of the audience, it is likely that such a procedure resulted in more than one biased court and presented an opportunity for bribery.[22] Testimony from the Republican period confirms that bribery and corruption were common among the jurors of the Late Republic, which explains Cicero's frequent digressions concerning jurists' moral obligation to adhere to traditional Roman values.[23]

Whether in legal or political disputes, popularity with audiences was not sought simply for reinforcing an advocate's ego but for more concrete, personal gain. Orators such as the Gracchi, Cicero, and even Caesar clearly revealed that powerful political careers could be established and sustained by recognition as a speaker. With political power moving toward the lower classes, orators began to secure widespread support which traditionally was restricted to individuals of wealth, military strength, and patrician influence. The source for attaining such support came from the development of a favorable public image.

Image-Construction and the *Vir Bonus* Personality

From the early Republic of Cato the Elder to the early Empire of Quintilian, Roman orators were tempered by the moral implications of "the good man [*vir bonus*] speaking well."[24] Public recognition associated with this concept provided a strong temptation for advocates to concentrate on a favorable public image and not the moral realities of the maxim.[25] Consequently, the appearance of a *vir bonus* image became important for personal gain, particularly in litigation. Composing an oration, then, became the occasion to enhance one's image by allowing the values articulated to become synonymous with one's character. The speech became the manifestation of the advocate's character and thus a forceful medium to indirectly enhance integrity. Thus an examination directed toward understanding the practicalities of promoting image—one which counters Plato's and Aristotle's concept of character—can unearth the significant impact which the advocate's personality had upon Roman discourse.

Greek rhetoricians labeled the concept of the speaker's character *ethos*, and Romans—who possessed no single word equivalent—Latinized the Greek term. Quintilian believed that *ethos* not only had no word equivalent but also no concept equivalent and considered *ethos* most similar to the Latin concept of *mores*, or the moral make-up of an individual.[26] Although familiar with the concept, Cicero never used the term *ethos* in his rhetorical treatises but did identify related character traits in successful orators.[27]

One character trait which Cicero frequently associated with advocates was *dignitas*. Cicero considered *dignitas* the mark of a person's breeding, a quality associated with virtuous conduct and pristine values.[28] He believed further that the moral obligations of *dignitas* entailed a duty toward justice and loyalty to the State.[29] But Cicero often seemed to be more concerned with the image of *dignitas* than the morality it implied since he admitted that the chief benefit of *dignitas* was its reward of public office, acquired by meritorious service.[30] Cicero's views were well expressed in a letter to Gnaeus Plancius: "If *dignitas* means that you should have solid opinions about public affairs, and to have them approved by 'good men,' my *dignitas* prevails. If, however, *dignitas* means you are able to execute your opinions or just to defend them by free speech, then indeed there is no vestige of *dignitas* left in me."[31]

Another term which Cicero used in discussing the character of popular advocates was *auctoritas*, or the forceful weight of an individual's personality. Like *dignitas*, *auctoritas* was associated with an orator's morality and public image; it was a type of long-range *ethos*. Cicero distinguished Cato Uticensis for this quality and believed that such a trait, acquired through experience and manifested particularly in later life, was "the summit of old age."[32] Although it is difficult to draw an exact correlation, the praise Cicero expressed for Cato Uticensis indicates that *auctoritas* was the manifestation of a *vir bonus* image that was at least partially acquired through a sustained reputation for public distinction and service.

Romans had several ways of securing credibility. Being born into a noble patrician family, acquiring fame as a victorious general, and serving the city with a long career in politics were all media for enhancing one's respect in Roman society. To these conventional avenues of social recognition must be added an illustrious career in advocacy. Advocates frequently utilized legal proceedings as an arena in which to demonstrate a *vir bonus* image.[33] Defending causes, protecting Rome from internal enemies, and preserving justice and harmony were laudable tasks. But the opportunity to exploit judicial proceedings was particularly evident on the side of the prosecution. Although defense implied an inherent nobility, the prosecutor could also be lauded if he appeared as an incorruptable guardian of public morality.[34] An examination of Cicero's prosecution speeches attests to an attempt to portray such an image.[35] A successful portrayal depended on the prosecutor's ability to dissociate himself from the criminal charged. A conviction would not only confirm the prosecutor's image as a defender of civic morality but would also so estrange him from similar causes that he would serve as an antimodel to any subsequent illegal act.

Court victories preserved popularity. More importantly, however, the sustained testimony and index of one's character were the narrative accounts of these trials. Thus, while the immediate audience witnessed victory secured, the distanced audience (of the posttrial publication) read an apologia. In essence, then, the posttrial published "speech" served to coexist the act of discourse with the quality of the advocate; the act became synonymous with the advocate. A public who viewed Cicero's arguments as virtuous was inclined to associate those qualities with his nature and view him as a virtuous man, a *vir bonus*. Coexisting the argumentative act with the essence of the advocate made the posttrial compositions rhetorical documents to the distanced audience. The intent of this written discourse, however, was not to win a trial but rather to win popularity by defending shared values. The trial became the instrument to secure the approval of the larger audience by indirectly arguing to establish a *vir bonus* image.

Cicero's Manipulation of the *Vir Bonus* Image: An Appeal to the Distanced Audience

As a *novus homo*, or "new man" whose ancestors had never held a Senatorial office or the consulate, Cicero gained considerable prestige by successfully prosecuting Gaius Verres for extortion during his governorship in Sicily.[36] In securing the decision against Verres, Cicero defeated the defense advocate Quintus Hortensius Hortalus, which placed him among the ranks of superior forensic orators. Even a cursory survey of the Verrine Orations (*In Verrem*) leaves little doubt about Cicero's serious commitment to the Sicilian cause and the thoroughness of his research and preparation. Cicero's effort exemplified the conscientiousness and industry which brought forth a success.[37]

Cicero's use of documents, testimony, and logical analysis in the *In Verrem* were presented to evoke a certain response from his listeners: Gaius Verres is a travesty to the Roman value system and ought to be punished. The importance of this line of reasoning is evident in the ethical considerations and *vir bonus* image which Cicero emphasized to his listeners throughout the trial. His prosecution of Verres could be interpreted as an attempt to utilize the forces of justice and equity for the preservation of the state. Positioning himself as a champion of the Sicilian cause, Cicero characterized his advocacy as a way to forestall a possible revolt or increased discontent in Rome's oldest province. By his method of prosecution, Cicero was considered a *vir bonus*—a good man who employed sanctioned methods of saving an otherwise stable society from anarchy.

Cicero's defense cases—particularly those presented during the height of his political career—also provide clear examples of his consideration of ethical issues and demonstration of a *vir bonus* image. Such characteristics appear in his forensic rhetoric during the time of his consulship and before his exile because of his increased involvement and influence in party politics. As early as 63 B.C., the *Populares*—under the leadership of men such as Julius Caesar—began to reinstate themselves as the political force which Sulla and the *Optimates* had crushed two decades earlier. In an attempt to contest the power of the Senate, the tribune Titus Labienus (almost certainly under the auspices of Caesar) prosecuted an established senator, Gaius Rabirius, on a charge of treason.[38] The alleged crime had actually occurred almost four decades earlier, when Rabirius supposedly murdered the tribune Lucius Saturninus, who had been instrumental in inciting a mob insurrection.[39] Fearful of chaos, the Senate then issued a *senatus consultum ultimum*, which declared a state of emergency; a number of radicals were killed while the riot was being suppressed.[40] The resulting *Pro Rabirio Perduellionis* became less an indictment of Rabirius than a challenge to the legal right of the *Optimates* to invoke the *senatus consultum ultimum*. As R. A. Bauman affirms, "the Populares were anxious to challenge the validity of the *sc. ultimum*. . . . They wanted to have the extreme decree pronounced on by the people."[41] The case was tried before a commission of two jurors or *duumviri*, one of whom was Caesar.[42]

Cicero's strategy in the *Pro Rabirio Perduellionis* was to stress the ethical and social issues of his case by doing rhetorically to the *Populares* what had been done physically to the insurgents four decades earlier: to remove any support by allying all social forces to the Senatorial Order. Cicero had a timely advantage in implementing this strategy because the case took place while he was consul.[43] His arguments rested on the belief that a conviction of Rabirius would mean "that hereafter the authority of the Senate, the sovereignty of the consul [and] the accord of good people would be powerless against the ruin and destruction of the state."[44] He argued further that this social disruption would provoke chaos and threaten the welfare of the Republic.[45] Consequently, such a threat prompted his defense not only as an advocate but as a consul guarding the stability of the state.[46] With this strategy, he was able to both stress the ethical issues of the case and ally his *auctoritas* and *dignitas* as a consul with his *vir bonus* image as an advocate; that is, he utilized the force of his political power and public image to further stress his arguments. Cicero did not deny Rabirius' crime but rather defended it.[47] Furthermore, he demonstrated how all political groups had rallied against the insurgents: *Populares* such as Gaius Marius, the *nobiles* of the Senate, the *equites*, the *tribuni aerarii*, "and the men of all remaining Orders who at that time took up arms in behalf of common liberty."[48] Cicero's strategy presented a *concordia ordinum* which united all classes into common approval of Rabirius' actions and diminished the effectiveness of certain men to alienate class factions.

An interesting example with which to compare his demonstration of ethical considerations and the *vir bonus* image occurred in his defense of the consul-elect Lucius Licinius Murena in 63 B.C. Indicted on a charge of electoral corruption through bribery, Murena was prosecuted by two distinguished advocates, Marcus Cato Uticensis and Servius Sulpicius Rufus, and two unknown advocates, Servius Sulpicius and Gaius Postumus.[49] Murena, however, was more than adequately represented by Cicero, Hortensius, and Marcus Licinius Crassus.[50] The *Pro Murena* took place during Cicero's consulship and in the midst of the Catilinarian conspiracy. In short, these forensic deliberations took place during a chaotic period, and Cicero recognized that this climate offered the advantage of a political dimension to his position.

Although Cicero's major task was to refute the charge of Murena's alleged *ambitus*—which he never actually confronted—he did attempt one strategy that is significant in understanding his perception of his audience(s). Cicero defended Murena not as an advocate but as a consul.[51] His strategy, although obvious, was quite shrewd. Murena, Cicero, and Hortensius were all associated with the consulship, and each of these men would represent a certain amount of public authority. Cato and Sulpicius Rufus, neither of whom had attained the consulship, relied more on their private reputations and skill as advocates.

Cicero attempted to secure the court's decision by mocking the legal profession and forensic rhetoric. He noted Murena's value to society as a military leader and an elected consul, admiring the "*summa dignitas*" of a consul "to be able, by deliberation and eloquence, to influence the minds of the Senate, people and those who judge."[52] In addition, Cicero argued that "there can be no *dignitas* in so shallow a skill [forensic rhetoric], for the matters are trivial, being almost completely concerned in individual letters and punctuations of words."[53] Cicero further argued that justice frequently was not served but was perverted by shrewd advocates who could never attain the distinction of consuls.[54] According to Cicero, "no one ought to be considered a wise man in that knowledge which neither has any power anywhere outside Rome nor at Rome when cases are deferred."[55] Cicero portrayed himself as postponing his consular duties and demeaning himself by engaging in the wranglings of the courts and not without clarifying that "those orators who were unable to excel, fall into the study of law."[56]

It appears from the *Pro Murena* that Cicero had little reluctance in publicly decrying the profession from which he earned his initial fame. Furthermore, his praise of the military over oratory was in direct opposition to his subsequently expressed opinions in *De Oratore*.[57] Most importantly, however, Cicero recognized the influence of his own *auctoritas* and *dignitas* as consul and did not hesitate to capitalize on this advantage. His strategy was pragmatic and expedient. Yet the argument he advanced in the *Pro Murena* indicated the inconsistency of dismissing the profession which he elevated in theory as the ethical guardian of the State.

Conclusion

Chaim Perelman and L. Olbrechts-Tyteca, the Belgian language philosophers, maintain that "a symbol can play an important role in the presentation of premises as well as in the body of argumentation."[58] This observation reflects the symbolic representation of the *vir bonus* image in Roman legal rhetoric for both the immediate and distanced audiences. Those who constantly strove to present themselves as "good men" speaking out against injustice frequently established themselves as symbols or personifications of the normative ethics of their culture: a standard dictated by their listeners. Advocates like Cicero became the very premises for their arguments, for they "symbolized" themselves as spokesmen for values lauded by their audience. They used their oratorical skills to gain approval with the listeners who gathered to judge and observe the argument. After the proceedings were concluded, the composed text of the speech provided another dimension to enhance an advocate's *vir bonus* image. These published speeches functioned as extensions of personality—sustained, paradigmatic recordings of causes championed for the larger public good. Distanced audiences viewed the cases (*post facto*) in a larger social context and were inclined to extend the advocate's mission beyond the particulars of the trial to the championing of society. It is difficult to read Cicero's orations and not make such extensions and more difficult to believe that these extensions were not intentional when composed.

The symbolization and establishment of character as premises for arguments provide insight of significant import for understanding audiences. The notion that conclusions are not binding unless premises are agreed upon is an acknowledged concept governing analytic thought. The *vir bonus* image examined here indicates that the morality and credibility of the orator was a force in argumentation; he was the actual starting point for his argument, the symbolized axiom of his logic. As a culture-bound phenomenon, the rhetorical process operates in the realm of metaphysics and consequently advances arguments that are probable rather than analytic. Yet speakers who successfully portrayed a *vir bonus* image strove for unequivocal acquiescence to their arguments—as in the acceptance of analytical propositions—with the tacit notion that their arguments derived from a character of unquestionable virtue. The *vir bonus* image became the unobtrusive premise for the proper course of action, which was then demonstrated through argumentation. Unfortunately, examples from Cicero's own rhetoric indicate that such a condition encouraged rhetors to stress the appearance of virtue over the realities of the moral commitment which it implied. Consequently, the notion of *vir bonus* came to mean more than the simple aggregate of acts which an individual actually performed but rather the appearance of such behavior—whether or not such behavior was genuine.

Cicero's recognition of the importance of the audience, his sensitivity to the impact of a favorable image, and his realization of how forensic compositions could be a source of power in Roman society have important implications for understanding the relationship between oral and written composition. First, audience is central to composing rhetorical argument, but there are different dimensions of audience. The immediate audience—particularly the public—appreciated the histrionic and emotive techniques that made such wranglings entertaining, and Cicero was shrewd enough to seek favor by appealing to their instincts. Yet in the heat of oral argument Cicero also had to satisfy the listeners who sat as judges and rendered legal decisions. While these listeners were not immune to his extralogical techniques, they had expectations for argument that differed from the crowds' and that also had to be taken into consideration. These two dimensions were important to the immediate situation, but Cicero also recognized the third dimension of audience, the distanced audience who would read the speeches after the trials. For these individuals the published speeches were inscribed records, stories which provided lessons in eloquence and values. Pragmatic cases portrayed as displays of enduring values permitted Cicero to appear as a champion, a guardian of Roman virtues.

Cicero's speeches had several functions. The most obvious is winning the trial. Cicero's published speeches, however, served another function which had importance beyond the trial. They became narrative accounts of events, dramatizations revealing a clash of issues and values. The importance of these documents are analogical and illustrative; they enabled Cicero to articulate values and causes that had political and social implications. While Cicero's forensic rhetoric is driven by audience, his arguments serve to secure decisions and (eventually) to enhance his credibility outside the courts of Rome. The published speeches—the literate monologues dramatizing Cicero's argument—function as the medium of power, the conduit for a permanent statement of his larger argument about political and social conditions.

5

The Verrine Orations

The Verrines enshrined a victory which greatly enhanced Cicero's reputation and strengthened his credentials as an aspiring statesman.

Thomas N. Mitchell, Cicero: The Ascending Years

For centuries Cicero's prosecution of Gaius Verres has endured as a paradigm of eloquence in legal argumentation. Cicero's popularity as an advocate—which was given impetus largely by the success of this prosecution—helps to explain the success of the *In Verrem*. Yet audiences change over time and across cultures, and other, more enduring reasons need to be provided if we are to understand why the *In Verrem* persists far beyond the concerns which initially motivated it. The merits of the *In Verrem* as oral argument include its literate style, which makes it an enduring illustration of eloquence. A sensitive examination of this unique literate style will reveal a great deal about Cicero's sustained influence as well as the relationship of oral and literate discourse which fostered its preservation.

In the spring 1982 issue of *Central States Speech Journal* Donovan J. Ochs provided readers with a cogent analysis of Cicero's forensic arguments against Gaius Verres; Ochs' thesis is that several of Cicero's oral arguments against Verres were essentially neither oral nor argumentative but a contrived "literary fiction" of the actual trial.[1] Ochs correctly indicates that only the initial orations were actually presented in court and subsequently revised for publication.[2] That is, Cicero presented some form of the *Divinatio* and *Actio Prima* before Verres, presumably because he realized his conviction was imminent, fled into exile and was condemned *in absentia*.[3] Cicero, however, published the five undelivered "orations" of the *Actio Secunda* as if they had been delivered in court.[4] Thus, several "orations" composed as legal arguments were never delivered but served, according to Ochs, "as springboards into [Cicero's] expostulations."[5] Ochs' essay explains why Cicero's *In Verrem* has persisted as a model in two respects: as an embellished and stirring persuasive argument, and as a paradigm of Latin literary prose. Ochs' analysis also reveals that Cicero's "rhetorical detailing" is a form of "narrative suasion" which, while obviously incompatible with the conventional mode of Roman forensic argument, is doubtlessly effective literature to an audience far removed from (but far more encompassing than) those few who were present to hear the oral arguments of the proceedings.[6]

Ochs points to yet another implication of this artifact of discourse. The *In Verrem* is unique in that we know which orations were delivered and which were published as fictive. Moreover, as Ochs correctly indicates, even the heuristic structures for such arguments—the organizational patterns of oral argument treated under the canon of *dispositio*—are fixed with certainty and accounted for thoroughly in Cicero's *De Inventione Rhetorica*.[7] Thus an analysis of the *In Verrem* provides insight into differences and similarities in the heuristics of oral and written rhetorical composition within a piece of discourse.

Oral and written expression were so inextricably bound in ancient discourse that its unity was an unquestioned presumption upon which theories of rhetoric were developed. Several forces contributed to the establishment of this presumption. Ancient Greeks—almost to the point of exclusivity—never learned to read silently. Consequently, the act of composing necessitated oral and written expression as a single phenomenon. The preeminence of the spoken word, the unity of oral and written discourse through the practice of reading aloud, and the rare ability to read silently are discussed in several works.[8] From another perspective, writing in ancient Greece was not only produced and understood through orality but was intended to be presented orally.[9] The debate over the varying degrees of literacy in antiquity continues, but it is safe to claim that literacy was far from commonplace and public documents were frequently presented at social events where they were read to audiences or at private symposia.[10] Given these conditions, there is little wonder why theories of rhetoric would not advance techniques which would sever the senses and conceptual processes involved in writing, reading, and speaking. This unity would be particularly evident in the production of such forms of rhetoric as forensic argument, which was implicitly intended for both hearing and publication. In fact, the history of early Greek logographers such as Lysias—particularly as revealed in the *Phaedrus*—illustrates this unity of composing argumentative discourse both for oral and written presentation.[11]

Despite the unity of oral and written rhetoric, we know from contemporary views of rhetoric that oral and written composition developed as separate genres with respective theories of rhetoric which are only now being reapproached. Unquestionably, our knowledge of how and when this separation emerged would provide valuable insight into the shift of epistemological presumptions resulting in varying modes of discourse. A shift in argumentative composition is particularly evident in Roman litigation, which not only moved considerably beyond the emerging notions of Hellenic forensic rhetoric mentioned above but had considerably refined legal procedures. Fortunately, there is one extant case known to have been composed for both oral argument and written composition as exclusive events: Cicero's *In Verrem*. Cicero's prosecution of Gaius Verres is an excellent model for study because it is a complete set of orations on a subject requiring proficiency in formalized forensic argument, which presumes a systematic process for structuring a case.

Heuristic Components of *Dispositio* in Ciceronian Rhetoric

The orations which compose Cicero's *In Verrem* are divided into three groups: the *Divinatio*, the *Actio Prima*, and the *Actio Secunda*. Cicero's procedure for ordering cases—which was the only schematic method he advanced in his *rhetorica* prior to the *In Verrem*—is presented in his *De Inventione Rhetorica*, which provided the heuristics for the structuring of argument in the West for over thirteen centuries.[12] In this theoretical treatise, Cicero established and discussed extensively his heuristic procedure for structuring argument: *exordium, narratio, partitio, confirmatio, reprehensio, digressio,* and *conclusio.*[13] In this respect, Cicero's writings offer us a unique opportunity to compare theory with practice; that is, a comparison of his theories of structuring argument—as seen in the *De Inventione Rhetorica*—with his *In Verrem* should provide a profitable basis for comparison between theoretical postulates and practical application and the relationship between oral and written expression.

Cicero divided the *exordium* into two parts, introduction or *principium* and insinuation or *insinuatio.*[14] Excluding a completely hostile audience, the usual function in the *exordium* was to win the good will of the listeners. The *narratio*, the second division of the Ciceronian structure, served as the expository section of the oration by relating the events warranting charges.[15] There were three types of *narratio*: *genus*, which encompassed only the topics of the case and the reason for the dispute; *digressio*, which extended the action beyond the limits of the actual charge, often to amuse the listeners, indict an opponent, or develop a comparison; and *genus est remotium a civilibus causis*, which treated subject matter that in no way related to the case. *Partitio*, the third division, had two forms: *aperio/controversia*, which concentrated on explaining the areas of agreement and disagreement with an opponent; and *expositio*, which ordered the matters to be argued into a coherent pattern.[16] The Ciceronian *partitio* was used to clarify the argument in the minds of the listeners. *Confirmatio*, the fourth division, established the likelihood of asserted charges from two sources: persons or *ex personis* and actions committed or *ex negotiis.*[17] *Reprehensio*, the fifth component in the structuring of Ciceronian argument, employed the same rhetorical strategies as the *confirmatio* but with the emphasis on counterargument.[18] Cicero maintained that "an argument that can be confirmed from some *loci*, can be refuted from the same *loci*."[19] *Digressio*, an optional division, was often used to amplify some area not directly related to the subject but helpful in persuading the listeners.[20] Lastly, the *conclusio* or *peroratio* ended an oration in three ways: *enumeratio* or summary, *indignatio* or exciting ill will against an opponent, and *conquestio* or moving the listeners to pity and sympathy.[21] From the categories of the *De Inventione Rhetorica*, the lines of argument that Cicero employed in his prosecution against Verres can be examined in order to determine their relationship to his theoretical heuristic patterns. The following analysis reconstructs the forensic arguments based on these heuristics of *dispositio* for legal composition. Departures or omissions from this formula are noted so that the modalities of expression become apparent and indicate any separation or specialization between oral and written composition.[22]

The Structuring of the *In Verrem*

	Divinatio
	Exordium
	I. A number of great champions have helped Sicily in the past.
principium	II. Sicily has seen fit to choose men.
	III. I have a duty to honor Rome.
	IV. This case is actually a defense of principles.
	Narratio
	I. This case requires that a capable and honest man prosecute.
genus	II. Two main considerations are present:
	A. Whom do the sufferers most desire?
	B. Whom does the defendant least desire?
	Partitio
	I. A Sicilian ought to have the right to defend his people under normal conditions.
aperio/controversia	II. The majority of Sicilians desire me and not another Sicilian.

Confirmatio

ex negotiis

I. The winner of the *Divinatio* must have the essential qualities of a prosecutor.
   A. He must possess an upright and blameless character.
   B. He must have firmness and honesty.
   C. He must possess qualities as a speaker.

ex personis

II. I have come with more popular support than Caecilius.

Reprehensio

I. Caecilius says the case ought to be prosecuted by one who has suffered most.
   A. I represent all Sicilians.
   B. Caecilius has not really suffered since he is Verres' *questor*.
II. Caecilius says that since he was Verres' *questor* he has information available.
   A. Our sacred custom frowns on a *questor* prosecuting his *praetor*.
   B. Caecilius could also destroy documents that would link him with Verres.

Digressio

I. Think of our forefathers' tradition.
II. Remember the responsibility of the Senatorial Order.

Conclusio

I. I have everything to lose if I fail, Caecilius nothing.

conquestio

II. If Caecilius is chosen over me Rome will know why.

Actio Prima

Exordium

I. All believe that the courts will never convict any man, no matter how guilty, if only he has money.
   - A. Efforts are now being made to fan the flame of Senatorial unpopularity *(principium)*
   - B. I oppose these efforts.

II. I have never sensed such grave danger to the Republic.

Narratio-Confirmatio

I. Verres committed many grievous acts as governor of Sicily.
   - A. He committed extortion for personal gain. *(genus)*
   - B. He committed unjust treatment toward allies.
   - C. He committed torture and execution of Roman citizens. *(digressio)*
   - D. He left cities defenseless to pirates.
   - E. He stole works of art.
   - F. He committed adultery and other shameful carnal acts.

II. Verres treats these crimes and the trial as a farce.

III. Verres has a plan to be illegally acquitted.
   - A. He will attempt to bribe the court.
   - B. Hortensius will be next year's consul and will virtually control politics with the Metelli.
   - C. Marcus Metellus will replace Glabrio as head of the Extortion Court. *(genus est remotium a civilibus causis)*
   - D. Electors were bribed by Verres against my election as *aedile*.

IV. When all this failed Verres adopted a new plan.
   A. He attempted to bribe court members.
   B. He attempted to stall the case until his corrupt court could gain office.

Partitio

I. Your plan, Hortensius, is a long trial.

aperio/controversia

II. My plan is a short initial address and a speedy trial.

Digressio

I. For fifty years the Equestrian Order has maintained an unblemished record of law courts.
II. Since the Senatorial Order has taken over the court's bribery is everywhere.
III. Heaven has granted us the opportunity to correct this situation with this trial.

Partitio

expositio

I. I shall engage in a somewhat different method of prosecution.
   A. The charge will be stated first.
   B. Supporting evidence will follow.
   C. Witnesses will then be called.
II. This method is not without precedent.

Confirmatio

I. Supporting evidence will be given in the following orations.

[none offered]

II. No persons or evidence will be presented now.

Reprehensio

[No explicit *Reprehensio* is presented.]

Digressio

[The *Digressio* occurs earlier in the oration.]

Conclusio

[No formal peroration was presented by Cicero beyond an expression of gratitude.]

Actio Secunda: Speech I

Exordium

I. The Senatorial Order is entrusted with a great responsibility.

principium — II. Many events have happened within the nine days.

III. Hortensius has attempted to block the proceedings.

insinuatio — IV. Verres has lived a life of crime.

Narratio-Confirmatio

I. Verres has committed numerous offenses throughout his life.

A. He fled from Carbo.

narratio: digressio — B. He was in league with Sulla.

C. He had Philodamus and his son killed.

confirmatio: ex personis et ex negotiis — D. He confiscated wills and treasures.

E. He extorted corn.

F. He issued unjust edicts.

II. There are numerous examples to supplement my charges.

Partitio

[No direct *Partitio* was presented.]

Confirmatio

[Confirming evidence was not divorced from the *Narratio* but incorporated into each instance.]

	Reprehensio
	[There was no refutation of opposing arguments.]
	Digressio
	[The entire speech did not specifically deal with the charge of extortion. There was no single marked *Digressio* in the speech other than occasional asides throughout the oration.]
	Conclusio
enumeratio	[There was no formal *Conclusio*, merely an end to the statement of facts.]
Actio Secunda: Speech II	
	Exordium
	I. I have come as the champion of the Senatorial Order.
principium	II. Sicily is the first and best province of Rome.
	A. She is the leading producer of grain.
	B. She adheres to stern Roman tradition.
insinuatio	III. Verres is the first man against whom their cities have officially sent witnesses to testify.
	Narratio-Confirmatio
	I. Verres distorts wills.
genus/digressio	
	II. Verres manipulates court procedure for his own ends.
digressio	III. Verres steals numerous articles of art.
	IV. Verres uses unethical conduct in conducting trials for capital offenses.
digressio	V. Verres committed numerous other judicial violations.

Partitio

[No clear section of the speech was given to illustrate either areas of agreement with opponents or the matters to be discussed.]

Reprehensio

I. Verres believes Sicilians are enemies.
   A. The Sicilians oppose Verres.
   B. The Sicilians do not oppose Rome.

Confirmatio

I. Verres exports contraband goods.

ex personis and *ex negotiis*

II. Verres uses the name "Verrucius."

Digressio

[There was no set place in the oration where a *Digressio* occurs.]

Conclusio

I. Hortensius has no lines of defense for Verres.

indignatio — II. Verres is devoid of Roman values.
   A. He lacks respectability.
   B. He lacks bravery.
   C. He is not good-natured.

Actio Secunda: Speech III

Exordium

principium — I. I prosecute Verres for the values held dear by Rome.

insinuatio — II. Why does Hortensius defend Verres?

Partitio

expositio — The speech will be divided into three parts.

Narratio

I. Verres has committed extortion through the illegal taxation of the corn-tithe.

	II. Verres has committed extortion
genus	through the unjust corn purchases.
	III. Verres has committed extortion through unlawful corn commutation.
	Confirmatio
ex negotiis	I. Verres changed the standard taxation system, breaking the law for his own benefit.
	A. Verres broke the law of Hiero.
	B. Verres issued special edicts.
ex personis	II. Verres sold tithe-rights illegally. [Numerous such cases were given.]
ex personis	III. Verres ill-treated those cities engaged in commutation.
	A. [Numerous cities are cited.]
	B. [Aetna and Leontini are covered in depth.]
	Reprehensio
	[No specific *Reprehensio* is offered.]
	Digressio
	[No specific *Digressio* is offered.]
	Conclusio
enumeratio	I. If men such as Verres are allowed to plunder, Sicily and Rome will be in economic ruin.
conquestio	II. We need to return the Sicilian farmers to their fields.
	Actio Secunda: Speech IV
	Exordium
insinuatio	I. No treasure was safe from Verres while he was in Sicily.
digressio	II. Verres argues that he purchased the statues.
	Narratio-Confirmatio
digressio	I. Verres has stolen shrines and art works.

digressio	II. Verres has given pirates sanctuary.
genus *confirmatio: ex personis*	III. Verres has robbed prominent men.
	Digressio
	I. Verres' greed, compared with Piso's honesty, mocks Roman values.
digressio	II. Verres has robbed many cities of their prized treasures.
	Partitio
	[No *Partitio* was indicated.]
	Reprehensio
	[No *Reprehensio* was indicated.]
	Conclusio
	I. The sarcastic eulogy given in honor of Verres by Messana is a mockery.
indignatio	II. The Verrine Festival is an affront to Roman tradition.
	Actio Secunda: Speech V
	Exordium
	I. There is a strong argument that Verres ought to be saved for military purposes.
insinuatio	A. Verres is not a good general.
	B. Verres has committed many crimes against the military.
	II. Verres has committed cruelties to Sicilians and Romans alike.
	Narratio-Confirmatio
digressio	I. Verres has had Sicilians and Romans beaten and flogged.
digressio	II. Verres has illegally made Messana build him a private cargo ship.
	A. Verres exempted men from service for a price.
confirmatio: *ex personis*	B. Verres forced ships to travel with few men.

digressio	III. Verres caused the loss of the fleet to the pirates.
digressio	IV. Verres unjustly executed the crew (Cicero charged Verres with destruction of the fleet).
digressio	V. No distinction was made between Romans and non-Romans (Cicero charged Verres with illegal persecution of Romans).
digressio	VI. Verres had Publius Gavius, a Roman citizen, crucified.
	Partitio
	[No *Partitio* was presented.]
	Reprehensio
	[No *Reprehensio* was presented.]
	Digressio
	[No *Digressio* was presented.]
	Conclusio
	I. May the gods render justice.
conquestio	
	II. My interests in prosecution have only been to defend the Republic.

Observations

While this study is not meant to summarize the *In Verrem*, a brief accounting of the structure outlined above should complement the observations that follow. The *Divinatio* is an oration given by an advocate to earn the right to prosecute. Cicero's *Divinatio* is a model of forensic composition with each of the seven components mentioned above apparent and in standard order. Similarly, the *Actio Prima*, the first oration of Cicero's prosecution, is also a meticulously composed oration which establishes charges, foreshadows procedures, and even anticipates constraints which the judges must overcome. In brief, both the *Divinatio* and the *Actio Prima* are highly structured arguments directed toward a specific audience.

A casual reading of the five orations which comprise the *Actio Secunda*, however, reveals a marked departure from the highly structured patterns which characterize the *Divinatio* and *Actio Prima*. While the first oration of the *Actio Secunda* discusses the actual crimes for which Verres was charged, it also chronicles numerous crimes of passion and serves as a prelude to digressions in subsequent orations. The second oration of the *Actio Secunda* is little more than a vilification of Verres' treatment of the Sicilians and a self-indulgent justification of Cicero's motives. The third oration of the *Actio Secunda* is an extended exposition of Verres' illegal taxation procedures, extortion practices, and unlawful corn commutation. While this oration approaches the point of litigation, its extended reporting constitutes a legal brief rather than a well-cast argument and would have been inappropriate for the dynamics of oral argument in Roman courts. The subsequent orations of the *Actio Secunda* amount to a sensational account of Verres' unethical conduct. Vivid examples dominate these speeches to the extent that the orations cease to be forensic arguments and become narrative scenarios. The fourth oration of the *Actio Secunda*, for example, is little more than a detailed rendering of Verres' plundering of Sicilian art treasures and complicity with pirates, which makes for excellent storytelling but curious argument. The fifth and final oration of the *Actio Secunda*, Cicero's portrayal of Verres' blatantly illegal crucifixion of the Roman citizen Publius Gavius, is an emotionally charged illustration of Verres' mockery of Roman values. Cicero's account ignores the structure of legal argument and constitutes a stirring (but irrelevant) culmination to his prosecution. In short, while the *Divinatio* and *Actio Prima* are paradigms of highly structured forensic argument, the five orations of the *Actio Secunda* are little more than detailed expositions which, although expressive, ignore the systematic structuring of forensic argument recommended by Cicero in theory.

Many of the latter orations in Cicero's *In Verrem* do not even closely conform to the standard heuristic structures of forensic oral argument. As a young advocate, Cicero would most likely not have moved too far from standard patterns, and orations which are known to have been delivered in some earlier version do follow the conventional format of oral argument. Cicero indicated in the *Actio Prima* that while he would modify the procedure for calling witnesses he would not deviate from the normal practice of prosecution and stressed that his subsequent orations would adhere even more closely to the traditional format of forensic oratory.[23] Yet it is obvious that a marked departure from the conventional form of argument does take place; in fact, the format evolves to almost purely literary exposition in the latter orations. One observation certainly can be drawn both from Ochs' essay and this study. We may well have in the *In Verrem* one of the prototypes illustrating George Kennedy's notion of *letteraturizzazione*—that is, the shift of rhetoric from its primary function of immediate, oral persuasion to rhetoric in a secondary function, the use of rhetorical techniques for effective literary expression.[24] Of course, in Kennedy's analysis these transformations often take place in different genres and even different historical periods. With the *In Verrem*, however, we have an instance of the phenomenon of *letteraturizzazione* occurring within one piece of discourse. Such an occurrence reveals an increasing specialization—and separation—of oral and written genres.

The initial orations of Cicero's *In Verrem*, particularly the *Divinatio* and the *Actio Prima*, demonstrate a consistent application of his heuristic procedure for structuring argument. Yet subsequent orations—especially the later orations of the *Actio Secunda*—indicate a decay in this schematic procedure. The *Divinatio* is a highly structured argument presented in the conventional heuristic pattern that is detailed in the *De Inventione Rhetorica*. Unfortunately, Cicero's *Divinatio* is the only extant specimen of its kind and the opportunity for comparison with any other artifact is unavailable.[25] It is clear, however, that this oration easily fits the heuristic pattern of arrangement for oral arguments. Later orations, however, present a markedly different compositional format, which indicates a clear departure from the formulaic structures that characterize oral argumentative composition.

The *Actio Prima* adheres to the conventional patterns of arrangement with some exceptions. The *Narratio* and *Confirmatio* are collapsed with an internal *digressio* inserted. A later *Confirmatio*, or statement of evidence, is promised but not offered. The *Partitio* occurs twice with a *Digressio* presented between them, which is understandable since the oration is one of a series, and Cicero was compelled to articulate his procedure and the responsibilities of the court clearly to his listeners. Lastly, no explicit *Reprehensio* nor formal *Conclusio* is presented. Again, these departures are understandable since this oration, as an *Actio Prima*, is one of a series. Yet we know that the latter arguments were never presented orally in court but were distributed for popular reading, and it is with this departure from an orally based composition to a series of argumentative compositions (which were not intended to be argued orally) that the greatest shift in heuristics occurs. As the summary of the five orations which compose the *Actio Secunda* reveal, there is almost a total departure from the heuristic structures which characterize oral argumentative composition. The arguments of the *Actio Secunda* repeatedly collapse the *Narratio* and *Confirmatio*, consistently omit or provide lip-service reference to formalized heuristic components, and diminish to the point of providing arguments which can only be characterized under *Digressio*.

There are several particular points in the *Actio Secunda* that differ markedly from the two previous orations, which were known to have been delivered orally. The first oration of the *Actio Secunda* avoided the *status* of the case, the charge of extortion, and instead concentrated on establishing facts about the activities and character of Verres. Similarly, the second oration in the *Actio Secunda* concentrated on various sensational activities Verres had engaged in as governor of Sicily and are presented more as a histrionic *exposé* than the carefully orchestrated argument which characterizes the *Divinatio*. In fact, it may have been Cicero's intent to underscore the indignation between Verres and the Sicilians which led to his placing the *Reprehensio* before the *Confirmatio*. The third argument of the *Actio Secunda* reveals only a semblance of the standard protocol for structuring argumentative compositions; the *Partitio* is inserted ahead of the *Narratio*, the *Reprehensio* and *Digressio* are omitted, and the body of the speech is taken up by a lengthy, informative *Confirmatio* which would have been perceived as a tenuous statement of facts if it were presented orally to Roman listeners. The fourth and fifth arguments of the *Actio Secunda* are typified by the excessive use of *digressio* within rubrics of argumentation and illustrate Cicero's tendency to collapse *Narratio* and *Confirmatio*. Cogent argument and meticulous attention to structure are replaced by sensational stories of Verres' pernicious crimes, culminating in his having a Roman citizen named Publius Gavius crucified. The lively scenes which Cicero colors throughout the latter orations offer vivid images of inhumanity to Roman readers but constitute poorly structured oral arguments.

Cicero's departure from the structures of *dispositio* for oral argument reveals several points of importance. First, several scholars have determined that the five orations which compose the *Actio Secunda* were never presented as oral argument but were written out after Verres fled into exile.[26] Consequently, Cicero may have considered these latter speeches little more than briefs composed and polished for publication and not requiring the rigorous schematization of the earlier, delivered speeches. If accurate, the implications of these distinctions for oral and written rhetoric are significant. Ancient rhetoric is based upon the notion of an inextricable binding of oral and written discourse. Yet the above findings reveal a marked distinction between those orations which were structured and composed for an immediate audience and those which were presented after the trial had passed to a more distanced audience of readers or listeners who gathered to hear what amounted to orally performed literature. Clearly, the latter orations reveal a departure from the heuristic protocol of argument to the extent that they are little more than strings of digressions. This phenomenon indicates that the close binding of oral and written rhetoric which is so evident in ancient Hellenic discourse was decaying by the time of Republican Rome and that different genres of composition were emerging even within the discipline of forensic argument. This instance provides a clear indication of that phenomenon.

Second, the close relationship between theory and application evident in the earlier orations may be fortuitous; Cicero never consciously adopted a formalized method for presenting his arguments. This possibility has strong points on both sides. On one hand, it is improbable that the presentation of the earlier orations fits the argumentative heuristic structure so consistently. On the other hand, Cicero did not hesitate to ignore theory in actual litigation—as the later years of his career reveal.[27] It is entirely possible that the departure of theory and application occurred at this early stage of his career, but it is doubtful that it occurred within an oration unless there was a conscious recognition of differences between oral and written composition of legal arguments. In either case, there is little doubt that Cicero had forsaken those tenets which he so carefully presented in such treatises as *De Inventione Rhetorica*.

Third and last, Cicero's deviation from formalized rhetorical techniques indicates that he did not restrict himself to one set theoretical protocol but would modify heuristic precepts of composition to the constraints of the case and, apparently, to the genre of oral and written or exclusively written forensic rhetoric. Such an explanation is probable when it is observed that he eventually modified the strict arrangement which he advocated in his youthful *De Inventione Rhetorica* and wrote in the *Partitiones Oratoriae* that he would adapt his entire plan of attack to the nature of a particular case.[28] In sum, Cicero possessed a knowledge and ability to use formalized systems of arrangement to structure his discourse but did not hesitate to modify his design to further the expediency or effectiveness of his cause. This modification, as revealed in the *In Verrem*, could be so radical in departure from theoretical precepts that heuristic structures directing the *dispositio* would be abandoned when the intent of composition shifted from oral to written argument or, in Ochs' term, to "narrative suasion."[29] Heuristic structures which were synonymous in oral and written rhetorical composition, particularly in argumentative discourse, were clearly beginning to be severed into discrete functions during the late Roman Republic and illustrate a trend which resulted in the bifurcation of rhetoric into mutually exclusive oral and written discourse. Cicero's *In Verrem* has two dimensions which warrant its preservation: initial orations which offered paradigms of effective legal argument and later orations which provided eloquent models of forensic rhetoric composed in a literate mode.

6

Legal Rhetoric in Theory, Practice, and Publication

The use of letters is to preserve vocal sounds and to return them to readers as something left on trust.

Quintilian, Institutio oratoria

Cicero's rhetoric became not only a guideline for effective oratory but a standard for literary expression to the point that "Ciceronianism" was an established mode of composition throughout the West.[1] Cicero's forensic speeches have served as models of advocacy to such an extent that today his statue stands at the very entrance to the Hall of Justice in Rome. Generations of Roman authors have taken Cicero as a model and have studied his rhetorical principles as standards to measure their craft. Ciceronian theory and the orations that conform to it became standards for literary expression. Those orations, however, that do not easily conform to rhetorical principles were frequently branded as inconsistent, expedient, or even hypocritical. What is apparent, however, is that many of Cicero's forensic arguments do not correspond to the theories he set forth in his rhetorical treatises. That such differences exist is apparent by reading the orations. Why such differences exist, however, is a key to understanding the relationship between oral and literate expression. The route toward this understanding requires, in turn, an understanding of Cicero's intentional discrepancy between theory and practice in legal rhetoric.

Rhetoric versus Oratory

According to Cicero and Quintilian, early Latin oratory was little more than rustic perspicuity which stressed diction; the Greek codification of a systematic oratory actually provided the impetus for a recognized "art" of rhetoric in Rome. [2] Schematic rhetoric never fully divorced itself from Greek tradition, however, and the anti-Hellenic sentiment of many Romans proved to be a strong deterrent to rhetoric's popular acceptance.[3] Cicero illustrates the curious views Romans had of Hellenic-based rhetorical theory and effective Roman advocacy. As a theorist, Cicero was the most influential rhetorician in the history of the Latin-speaking West and, prior to his career as an advocate, actually studied rhetorical theory in Athens, Asia Minor, and Rhodes from 79–77 B.C.[4] Cicero's own training in rhetoric led to clearly formed opinions about formal training in the discipline and its application in the courts of Rome. Cicero's praise of Greek rhetoricians, for example, was quite selective. He praised the type of Athenian rhetoric which he saw in Plato's argumentation but believed that many contemporary "Greeklings" sought controversy more than truth.[5] Excluding the teachers under whom he studied as a young man, Cicero rarely praised any rhetorician, let alone a Greek rhetorician, and never while he was pleading. His praise was limited for the most part to early Greek orators such as Demosthenes and Aeschines, primarily because they were men who used oratory for the benefit of the State.[6]

Similarly, Cicero had little use for sophistic pedantry, as is reflected in his *De Oratore* when Crassus—in answer to Sulpicius' question as to whether rhetoric was an "art"—asks if he ought to be considered "some sort of leisurely, jabbering, present-day Greekling, who is perhaps learned and educated."[7] Later in the dialogue, Catulus, discussing the necessity of practice, argues that he does "not need the help of some Greek teacher, who chants very common maxims to me when he himself has never looked upon the Forum or any law court."[8] Cicero's criticism of foppish rhetoric was not limited to the Greeks; in fact, the lack of practicality in schoolbook rhetorical exercises so annoyed Cicero that he even rejected his own *De Inventione Rhetorica* as the pedantic "notebook" of a boy.[9]

Cicero did not condemn rhetorical devices or rhetoricians who trained men for advocacy. He disdained those who encouraged a rhetoric which was of little benefit to society. Cicero's contempt for pedantic rhetoricians was most clearly evident in his *Orationes Philippicae*, particularly when he assassinated the character of a rhetorician named Sextus Clodius, whom he considered nothing better than a sophistic lackey to Mark Antony.[10] Cicero was particularly critical when orators failed to supplement their education with practical experience in the courts, but relied on schematic theories of armchair rhetoricians. As a successful orator who wrote about rhetoric, his own views and approach emphasized the philosophical bases of rhetoric and not the schematic approach of rhetoricians who preceded him. The majority of his works on rhetoric are inquiries about the principles underlying success in oratory—practical analyses of why and how argumentative strategies function in various situations. In essence, Cicero examined the nature of argumentative processes.

True to his sentiments about the utility of rhetoric, Cicero's theories of legal argument were direct and pragmatic. Often stressing broad principles of oratory, his own views were that no single plan of arrangement or style ought to be presented for every case.[11] In fact, Cicero believed that the legal style of speaking ought to be more "archaic," brief, and with a restricted use of rhythmical periods.[12] The primary concern of the advocate was not so much the discovery of facts, which he felt were relatively easy to acquire, but rather the treatment and adaptation of material.[13] Crassus, in *De Oratore*, was even concerned that the precepts he advanced would appear to be more difficult than they were in practice.[14] Cicero himself believed that rhetorical precepts in forensic argument could often be quite simple, as he indicated through Antonius in *De Oratore*: "One should say some introductory remarks, then explain the case, next one should prove it by strengthening one's defended positions and by refuting opposing arguments, finally one should wind up and conclude; the very nature of oratory commands this, but one should indeed determine just how one should compose those things which ought to be said for proving and explaining the case—that is indeed the most noteworthy characteristic of knowledgeable oratory."[15]

Rhetoric, to Cicero, did not create advocates but polished and strengthened whatever traits an individual possessed innately. The utility of Ciceronian rhetoric in forensic argument was that it emphasized listener behavior, speaker-image, and ability more strongly than the phraseology of recipebook schemes. Once an advocate began to understand these fundamental heuristics of litigation, he could analyze the specific nature of the case, the audience, and his role and draw from a variety of rhetorical strategies to persuade a specific group of listeners. The particular qualities which an orator possessed, recognized, and utilized in a case would partially determine his success. The mark of a successful advocate, then, was his ability to adapt arguments and rhetorical strategies which would have the greatest influence on an immediate, specific audience.[16] Cicero's precepts for a pragmatic rhetoric of the courts indicate that a successful forensic orator needed to possess the facilities to marshal superior arguments for an audience, an ability which was aided by—but not dependent upon—an understanding and application of formalized rhetorical theory. Realizing Cicero's pragmatic view of the nature of rhetoric serves as a basis for comparing the implementation of his strategies as an advocate with the precepts he espoused as a theorist and offers a reference point to explain why such differences occur.

Practice versus Theory

Whether by natural genius or practical training, Cicero clearly demonstrated proficiency in utilizing techniques associated with formal rhetorical training. Several extant orations illustrate his ability to structure quasi-logical argument—that is, cogent argument grounded in probability and intended for a particular audience.[17] One of the clearest examples of Cicero's application of rhetorical strategies occurred in his earliest existing defense speech, the *Pro Quinctio* in B.C. 81. The case was a private dispute over the property rights of a Gallic estate between Publius Quinctius, who inherited his brother Gaius' land rights, and his partner Sextus Naevius.[18] After a financial dispute between the partners, Naevius secured an edict from the *praetor* Burrienus and ejected Publius three days later. Publius, contesting the legality of the edict and the praetorian decision, entered a *sponsio* with Naevius—a mutual agreement that the loser of the case pay a stipulated amount to cover court costs.[19] Cicero concentrated on an analysis of the validity of the edict, which he summarily dismissed, and attempted to win the case by relying on arguments of probability, which were often presented through a series of rhetorical questions.[20] His primary method was to use arguments of probability and counterreasoning which shifted the burden of proof back to the prosecutor, Hortensius.[21]

Cicero's ability in probabilistic analysis was also demonstrated in refutation, as occurred in 80 B.C. with his *Pro Roscio Amerino*, a defense of Sextus Roscius on a charge of parricide.[22] The elder Sextus Roscius, a Sullan supporter, was murdered in Rome while his son was in Ameria. Cicero indicated that Titus Roscius Capito and Titus Roscius Magnus, both of whom had less than amicable relations with the father, desired his property along with Lucius Cornelius Chrysogonus, an influential freedman of Sulla. When the elder Roscius was mysteriously murdered, his son was accused of parricide by these three men.[23] Furthermore, Chrysogonus, allied with Capito and Magnus, attempted to take the property that the son would inherit by illegally placing the father's name on the proscription list that had been completed in the previous year.[24] Such a ploy would deny inheritance rights to the son and enable the three men to purchase the property at a fraction of its value.[25] No murder trials had been held for some time, so a large crowd came to witness Cicero's defense of Sextus Roscius against an unknown but "experienced accuser" by the name of Erucius. [26]

Cicero concentrated his defense on two points: refuting the assertion that Sextus Roscius committed parricide and presenting a countercharge against Titus, Magnus, and especially Chrysogonus. Cicero attempted to refute the charge of parricide by disclaiming the credibility of Erucius' charges. He summarily dismissed prosecution arguments as "improbable" assertions that not only differed from the truth but lacked proof and explained to his listeners that "the case centers on parricide; and rationale from the prosecutor has not answered why the son would have killed his father."[27] While dismissing the prosecutor's "idle conjectures," Cicero lampooned the accuser Erucius as "playing the fool" and mocked his ethics as a travesty to traditional Roman values.[28] His clearest demonstration of probable cause, however, occurred throughout the remainder of the oration, where Cicero sought to enhance his case by shifting the motive for murder back to the prosecution by establishing a *cui bono*, a concept popularized half a century earlier by Lucius Cassius, which attempted to establish "to whose advantage" the crime would be or, in this instance, who would most likely have profited from the murder.[29]

The forensic arguments discussed above illustrate Cicero's ability to apply formalized rhetorical techniques into quasi-logical arguments. Other orations, such as his *Pro Caecina* in 69 B.C., also provide excellent illustrations of counter-argumentation and legal interpretation.[30] Cicero's ability to apply rhetorical theory should not be surprising, considering his ability to adapt his philosophical training in ethics and dialectic to litigation. Cicero's extensive study in moral philosophy, antithetical reasoning, and probability provided obvious advantages in legal argument and complement his rhetorical training. The benefits of Cicero's eclectic education were realized because of his ability to apply esoteric philosophical and rhetorical principles to the pragmatics of legal argument. The cases discussed above illustrate that Cicero continually modified and adapted principles of logical argument to fit the situations. This pattern is evident not only in his legal speeches but in the general scope of his public oratory. Cicero saw the courts as a source of political power where cogent argument could not only secure a favorable decision in a case but indirectly be a means for advancing a particular political viewpoint.[31] The party politics and personal interest inherent in Roman legal argument would make adjusting rational arguments to particular audiences understandable. What is surprising, however, is Cicero's ability to ignore rhetorical and philosophical precepts when appropriate.

Emotive versus Rational Appeals

Although Cicero utilized established principles of rhetoric in his arguments, he would often attempt to appeal to the attitudes and prejudices of his listeners. In the *Pro Roscio Comoedo* (77 B.C.) Cicero, lacking strong evidence upon which to construct reasonable arguments, relied upon attacking the credibility of opposing arguments, advancing illogical or improbable positions, and implementing extralogical appeals. The case involved a property dispute stemming from settlement rights over a murdered slave named Panurgus.[32] Unable to present primary evidence or personal testimony, Cicero introduced a secondhand account of the proceedings through the evidence of two senators, Titus Manilius and Gaius Luscius Ocrea.[33] Although this was obviously hearsay, Cicero argued that such testimony actually held greater authority than the prosecution's primary evidence because of the character of his witnesses.[34]

In addition to such tenuous arguments, Cicero employed extralogical tactics to discredit opposing viewpoints. A major section of the oration was an admitted *digressio* lauding Roscius and lampooning Chaerea. "For when he portrays Ballio, that very perverse and lying brothel-keeper, he portrays Chaerea; that filthy, vile, perverted character portrayed him in his manners, nature and life. Who, therefore, would consider Roscius similar to him in deceit and malice; to me he seemed like a pimp, unless perhaps he noticed that he excellently imitated him in the character of a brothel-keeper."[35] Cicero advanced *ad personam* attacks against Fannius through probable argument.[36] Unlike previously mentioned orations, his claims were not supported by stringent analysis and testimony. Rather, his use of probability consisted of little more than lip-service ploys to imply the likelihood of claims which were not rationally established. In short, Cicero did have potentially strong arguments, but lacking adequate testimony and supporting evidence, he executed his strategy of discrediting the prosecution by advancing illogical assertions and relying on extralogical, *ad personam* attacks that violated the high morality which he supported in theory.

Another instance in which Cicero stressed extralogical appeals to secure conviction occurred in the *Pro Fonteio*, one of his first cases following the prosecution of Verres. Marcus Fonteius, a former *quaestor* in Gaul and *legator* in Spain, was prosecuted by the Gauls through Marcus Plaetorius for his misgovernment as *praetor*.[37] One strategy is readily apparent throughout the *Pro Fonteio*: an attempt to discredit the Gauls as a race inferior to the Romans. The charges against Fonteius included his misuse of funds for road work and his establishment of an unjust wine tax.[38] Both prosecution and defense based their arguments on testimony, the prosecution relying on Gallic witnesses and Cicero relying on Roman provincials and allies.[39] Since their testimonies conflicted, Cicero's strategy was to gain credence for his defense by arousing prejudice against the Gauls. Cicero admitted that he was departing from his "usual caution and carefulness"; he reminded the jurors of how the Gauls "waged harsh and long wars with the Roman people" and dismissed Gallic evidence as "barbarian testimony."[40] Consequently, he felt justified in informing the jurors of their moral and legal responsibility to disregard the attitude that "since witnesses testify, it ought to be believed without any hesitancy."[41]

The obligation Cicero stressed as sufficient cause for a prejudiced interpretation of conflicting testimony was inconsistent with his professed opinions in the prosecution of Verres. Throughout the *In Verrem* Cicero utilized the provincial testimony of Sicilians and incessantly warned the jurors of the need for objectivity. His strategy for the *Pro Fonteio* not only constituted an *ad personam* attack designed to stir Roman bigotry but also subordinated reasoned analysis and testimony in order to secure a decision. In essence Cicero was not above distorting a case in order to secure a decision. In fact, Quintilian maintained that Cicero was proud of such an ability and boasted when "he spread darkness itself upon the jurors in the case of Cluentius."[42]

Prior to his exile in 58 B.C., Cicero pleaded two defense cases: the *Pro Sulla* and the *Pro Flacco*. In both Cicero illustrated another extralogical strategy not uncommon in his forensic oratory—direct emotional appeal.[43] The cases involved different issues: in the former case Publius Cornelius Sulla was indicted for conspiring in the Catilinarian revolt, and in the latter case Lucius Valerius Flaccus was charged with misgovernment in Asia. In both the *Pro Sulla* and *Pro Flacco*, however, Cicero concluded by bringing his defendants' sons into the court and portraying them as "begging" (*orare*) and weeping for the lives of their fathers.[44] Although this tactic was hardly a novel approach, it indicated that Cicero would not hesitate to evoke the emotions of his listeners. It also showed that he would utilize extralogical arguments that could be drawn from the particulars of a case and incorporate any device that he thought would yield the desired response.

An interesting oration in which to compare Cicero's versatile manipulation of extralogical appeals is the *Pro Rabirio Postumo*

(54 B.C.). Rabirius was indicted on a charge of *repetundae* under the *Lex Iulia de Repetundis* when he was accused of aiding Gabinius in an illegal attempt to restore Ptolemy as King of Egypt—an act for which both Romans were handsomely bribed.[45] Rabirius was also a recognized affiliate of Caesar, whose power was—without question—a strong force in the party politics of 54 B.C. At one point in his defense, Cicero devoted an entire passage to praising Caesar and stressing his close relationship with Rabirius.[46] His strategy was to ally the two men so closely that a conviction of Rabirius would appear as an affront to Caesar. Cicero's tactic amounted to a threat to the jurors: "If one [Caesar] heard that a very dear friend was robbed of his integrity, he would neither bear it without great sorrow nor have lost that which he hoped could be recovered."[47] Cicero's extralogical appeal was a blatant attempt to prejudice the jurors through threats, and the precedent of Sulla's proscription lists was one consequence of offending a powerful leader which would be evident to jurors. Ironically, one of Cicero's first cases, the *Pro Roscio Amerino*, was a strong stand against the possible prejudices of authoritative leaders such as Sulla. Furthermore, as early as 69 B.C. Cicero had argued and admonished jurors throughout the *Pro Cluentio* to avoid prejudice.[48] Yet two orations of Cicero, the *Pro Flacco* and the *Pro Scauro*, indicated that he would employ prejudicial statements against Greeks, Jews, and Sardinians in order to discredit their testimony. And the *Pro Rabirio Postumo* clearly demonstrates that Cicero was not reluctant to capitalize on Caesar's *auctoritas* in order to secure a decision.

Practice and Posttrial Publication: A Perspective on Literate Models

The defense strategies discussed here indicate that Cicero employed a variety of methods to secure decisions, including quasi-logical, illogical, and extralogical arguments which were reinforced through his person, power, and reputation. In fact, Cicero admitted that he would adapt his beliefs and ethics to an individual case.[49] Cicero demonstrated cogent, rhetorical analysis through his use of probability and supporting evidence, particularly in the defense cases of his early career. He would often support his probable arguments with testimony, precedent, and such legal heuristics as the *cui bono* concept. Yet in spite of his theoretical insistence upon cogent argumentation and appeals to the ultimate law of reason, Cicero often used illogical and improbable argumentation and employed lines of analysis that would—perhaps intentionally—confuse his listeners and befuddle issues. Furthermore, Cicero relied on various extralogical appeals which were not advocated in theory. Such extralogical appeals often occurred in cases where his analysis appeared tenuous. During such cases, Cicero often kept his opposition off balance by shifting the burden of proof, discrediting opposing testimony, and introducing into the case irrelevant arguments which the opposition was encouraged to refute.

In theory, Cicero lauded the concept of a *vir bonus*: an individual who could safeguard the moral code of the State through an "honorable" system of litigation. Yet he was not above employing unethical tactics and often presented *ad personam* attacks against prosecutors, witnesses, and even forensic argument itself.[50] While he often pleaded for objectivity, Cicero would not hesitate to influence a decision—even to the extent of bringing crying children into the court—if it increased the possibility of a successful verdict. He incessantly demanded high ethical standards in courts, yet would prejudice jurors by threatening the wrath of Caesar if "justice" was denied or even lampoon opposing testimony with racial slurs if it meant winning a case.

In spite of the inconsistencies between established rhetorical theories, Cicero's various strategies indicate remarkable versatility, a capacity for adapting arguments to the nature of the occasion and listeners. Such a paradox may be resolved by observing the inherent difference between theory and practice. Cicero's ability in argumentation remains unquestioned. Yet when a case and its supporting evidence seemed tenuous, Cicero would forsake reason and advance illogical and improbable argument and extralogical methods which would distort the point at issue, shift the burden of proof, or pander to the prejudices of his listeners. Cicero demonstrated several qualities which he praised in theory, but he did not hesitate to forsake or compromise them if they diminished his chance to secure a decision. He did not feel obligated to idealistic theories drawn from rhetoric. He employed virtually any pragmatic strategy which would aid in securing a decision in his favor, regardless of the ethical implications. Above all else, Cicero's strongest quality was an ability to judge and adapt his position in the manner which he felt would be most advantageous and expedient. Recognizing this, we see little consistency between Cicero's theory of forensic rhetoric and his practice as an advocate. In fact, any consistency in Cicero's advocacy with the standards of his rhetorical works may have seemed to him merely fortuitous, and the numerous inconsistencies which he displayed were perhaps inconsequential or irrelevant to his primary obligations as a pleader. Admirers of Cicero's contributions may have hoped for greater consistency between his theory and practice. Yet it should be noted that several of his orations, often presented under the most difficult political and social conditions, have endured along with his theoretical works as exemplifying the best contributions to forensic argument.

Cicero's versatility in his legal argument offers us a better understanding of his attitude toward the relationship of theory to practice and, ultimately, the relationship between arguments given orally and published speeches presented to distanced readers. The immediate speeches require adaptation to the situation and adjustment to the listeners. No degree of posttrial revision could alter the tenor of those addresses without risking a loss of the orations' real identity. The published speeches had a different audience, an audience removed from the real event but sufficiently engaged to seek a reading. To this audience Cicero composed a literate fiction, coloring the address, refining the emotive and irrational appeals through pleas of ethical justification that would create dramatic scenarios. While it is likely that the core of Cicero's case and the basic line of his reasoning would have remained true to the actual event, the published speech provided an opportunity to justify such departures from reason which he supported in theory. It is striking that some of the most irrational passages are also the most stirring, so much so that a reader could easily fail to recognize them as nothing more than elegant appeals to prejudice or personal attack. Cicero demonstrated that he would deviate from idealized principles of rhetoric to secure a favorable decision. It seems just as likely that he may have used the published speeches—the literate versions and testimonials of his oral arguments—to modify those erroneous arguments which were immediately effective but not worthy of sustained praise, to cloak in penned eloquence what were shortcomings in theory. Thus the literate mode of Cicero's arguments provided the occasion to color the discourse of the trial while keeping those features which prompted readers to assume that the compositions were only published accounts of oral arguments and not, in reality, stylized recreations for a different, literate audience than those who sat listening in judgment at the Forum.

7

Conclusion: Orality and Literacy

It is primarily on his speeches, perhaps, that the literary reputation of Cicero has depended in recent times. . . . But how did the spoken word become literature?"

L. P. Wilkinson, The Cambridge History of Classical Literature

Numerous anecdotes have grown out of Cicero's legal wranglings but none more fitting to conclude this study than the one told by the eminent Roman historian Dio Cassius.[1] In a passage discussing an unusually tumultuous situation in the Republic, Dio tells of Pompey's strong-arm influence in Rome and how he marched into the court with his soldiers to observe Cicero's defense of Milo, who had been charged with the murder of Clodius. Seeing the court encircled with Pompey's soldiers, Cicero became so alarmed that he abandoned his carefully prepared composition, muttered only a few words extemporaneously, and was relieved when he finished. Cicero's good friend Milo was (of course) convicted and sent to Massilia in exile. A considerable time after the trial—when in a more relaxed mood—Cicero recomposed a speech he would have liked to have presented orally and sent it to his exiled friend, Milo. In a grand gesture of humor and integrity, Milo read the never-delivered-oration and wrote back to Cicero expressing his thanks that such an eloquent argument had never been spoken in court; otherwise, he might never have had the occasion to sample the fine fish of Massilia.

Conclusion

Cicero, naturally, did not publish his courtroom ramblings muttered in the presence of Pompey and his armed soldiers, but the undelivered written composition, the *Pro Milone*, is commonly acknowledged as one of Cicero's most eloquent masterpieces of legal rhetoric. If Dio's anecdote had been placed at the beginning of this work the depth of the relationship between Cicero's oral and literate modes of rhetoric and the meaning of these texts to their different audiences, might have been passed over with only a pejorative comment about Cicero's lack of fortitude. Yet if we look beyond his momentary failing of courage, we find a phenomenon whose initial appearance belies its complexity. Cicero's forensic orations have been available for centuries and have served as models of eloquence, evidence of Roman litigation, and statements of cultural values. While these uses of Cicero's forensic rhetoric remain unaltered, this study encourages a modified approach to the nature of those texts and reveals dimensions of communication which must be considered for a sensitive understanding of Cicero's rhetorical ability.

Cicero is widely recognized for his oratorical and literary skill. There are, however, relationships which have not been recognized previously but which are indispensable to our examination. We must recognize that a relationship existed for Cicero between his skill as a pleader and his competency as a composer. Cicero's abilities in speaking and writing functioned as confluent talents which raised his level of expression beyond any Roman standard. The legal profession in Rome was a predominantly oral phenomenon. Writing preserved laws and recorded events; issues and statements were made orally before particular audiences for specific occasions. Without oratorical skill no advocate could hope to gain any great measure of success. Possessing such ability not only earned Cicero a privileged status among advocates but was a source of power in Roman society. For Cicero, effective oral expression in the courts acted as a medium for public and eventually political recognition.

Cicero's extensive training in composition and his prolific written efforts provide an index of his control and range in writing. This skill facilitated his legal compositions and impressed listeners who, by all accounts, gave as much attention to how something was appealed as to the logic driving it. Cicero's literate mind provided a technology that facilitated reasoning and expression which, by degree, excelled his legal colleagues'. Yet to credit Cicero's "literate mentality" to the composing of arguments for the trial is to offer only partial credit. For generations these speeches have been preserved as our accounts of the trials, as specimens of oral argument. But these published speeches represent another rhetorical act. Cicero's speeches composed after the trial were actually seperate literary efforts. They appear as oratory and have the features of that Roman genre, but they are in fact stylized literary accounts. These published statements are not fiction, for they do reflect actual events, but it is fair to consider them as rhetorical interpretations. That is, Cicero's oral arguments were indeed acts of rhetoric, discourse intended to influence others in an event. The compositions later published as speeches were rhetorical literature, aesthetically contrived pieces of discourse that respond not to the particular situations they appear to address but function rather as larger, social statements. Making distinctions between the oral arguments as *rhetoric* and the posttrial literary compositions as *rhetorical* interpretations goes beyond merely labeling different acts with nouns and adjectives. The intent here is to distinguish the task and audiences in these respective acts of discourse as clearly as they doubtlessly were to Cicero.

Cicero's published speeches functioned as metaphors, cultural statements about conditions which transcended the immediate issues of litigation. They appeared direct and specific to a charge of injustice. However, many of the topics and conflicts Cicero chose to highlight were representative of social conditions so that his published compositions functioned as generalized criticisms of the prevailing conditions which Cicero's private letters reveal as personally distressing. These published speeches, then, were oblique responses to conditions, and his pleadings served as a medium for commentary. Generations of scholars and Latin teachers have used these legal orations as models of Latin eloquence and humanistic values; we realize now that our preservation of the orations in this way meets Cicero's intent. He recognized that his skill in composition could not only aid in the presentation of his oral delivery, for which he earned praise and advancement, but that his writing skills would perpetuate his personal influence by permitting the gist of his arguments to be cast in a larger social situation and function as a preserved and enduring response to conditions that the specific trials only reflected.

The generations immediately following Cicero's benefited from great literary figures. The Augustan Principate was enhanced by the artistic works of such luminaries as Virgil, Horace, and Livy. Each of these three writers saw fit to use their literary creations as media to express cultural values in harmony with Augustus' policies. Each individual was familiar with Cicero's efforts and perhaps recognized the many purposes written discourse could serve. Each of their literary efforts, while aesthetic or scholarly, were also rhetorical statements about their culture. Cicero's legal speeches foreshadowed this phenomenon by revealing the power such rhetorical literature could have in social interaction. The plasticity Cicero demonstrated in expressing his legal rhetoric set him apart from all other Roman advocates and, more importantly, illustrates what eloquent wranglings could result when a literate mind is sensitive to rhetorical conditions beyond those prompted by the immediate event. Cicero's unprecedented blend of orality and literacy and his awareness of multiple audiences established a paradigm that later Romans would model.

Notes

Bibliography

Index

Notes

1. The Pragmatics of the Roman Court

1. The exact relationship between Cicero's theory and practice is particularly tenuous in his forensic rhetoric, possibly because, as S. F. Bonner argues, few scholars have attempted the task of relating oratory and rhetoric to law: S. F. Bonner, "Roman Oratory," *Fifty Years (and Twelve) of Classical Scholarship*, ed. Maurice Platnauer, 2d ed. (Oxford: Basil Blackwell, 1968), 456. When attempts have been made to evaluate the theory and practice of his forensic rhetoric, the emphasis has been on either legal science or procedure and not advocacy: Emilo Costa, *Cicerone Giureconsulto*. Edizione Anastatica, vol. 1 (Rome: "L'Erma" de Bretschneider, 1964); A. H. J. Greenidge, *The Legal Procedure of Cicero's Time* (Oxford: Clarendon Press, 1901); Alain Michel, *Rhétorique et Philosophie chez Cicéron* (Paris: Presses Universitaires de France, 1960); J. Stroux, "Summum Ius Summa Inuiria" in *Romische Rechtswissenschaft und Rhetorik* (Potsdam: Stichnote, 1949).

2. Ronald Syme, *The Roman Revolution* (Oxford: Oxford University Press, 1963), 94.

3. Readers who wish to review background information about the legal developments of the Roman Republic and their impact on party politics are encouraged to consult H. H. Scullard, *From the Gracchi to Nero: A History of Rome: 133* B.C.–A.D. 68 (London: Methuen, 1963), *passim*.

4. Scullard, 86.

5. Plutarch, *Vitae Parallelae: Cicero* 2.

6. Plutarch, *Vitae Parallelae: Cicero* 2. For the fragments of Cicero's poetry see: *Ciceronis Poetica Fragmenta*. Recensuit Antonius Traglia. Fasciculus prior (Rome: Cas Editrice Gismondi, 1950). For an index to the fragments of Cicero's poetry see *Index Verborum Ciceronis Poeticorum Fragmentorum*, ed. John William Spaeth, Jr. (Urbana: University of Illinois Press, 1955). Cicero, *Pro Archia* 1.

7. Cicero, *Brutus* 305; *Tusculanae Disputationes* 1. 7.

8. Suetonius, *De Rhetoribus* 25.

9. Cicero, *De Optimo Genere Oratorum* 17–18.

10. Quintilain, *Institution oratoria* 10. 7. 30–31.

11. Plutarch, *Vitae Parallelae: Cato Minor* 23. While Cicero was clearly adept at this method of shorthand, Tiro was unquestionably an invaluable aid to his composition: Cicero, *Epistulae ad Atticum* 13. 32.

12. Evidently Cicero depended heavily on Tiro in many respects relevant to writing other than the transcription of oral arguments and arranging his books, and his affectionate letters to his freedman indicate that Cicero's literary productivity was hampered when Tiro was ill: Cicero, *Epistulae ad Familiares* 16. 14, 20, *et passim.*

13. Cicero, *Brutus* 91–93.

14. Cicero, *Brutus* 61.

15. Cicero, *Epistulae ad Atticum* 3. 12.

16. Suetonius, *De Rhetoribus* 26.

17. Cicero, *De Amicitia* 1.

18. Cicero, *De Legibus* 1. 13; *De Amicitia* 1.

19. Cicero, *Brutus* 307–8.

20. Cicero, *Brutus* 308.

21. Cicero, *Brutus* 311.

22. Cicero, *De Natura Deorum* 1. 6–7.

23. Aubrey Gwynn, *Roman Education from Cicero to Quintilian* (Oxford: Oxford University Press, 1926), 69.

24. Cicero, *Brutus* 306.

25. Cicero, *Brutus* 315.

26. Cicero, *Brutus* 315.

27. Dionysius of Halicarnassus, passage quoted by E. G. Sihler, *Cicero of Arpinum* (New Haven: Yale University Press, 1914), 57. Cicero, *Brutus* 315.

28. Cicero, *Brutus* 316.

29. D. A. Russell, *Greek Declamation* (Cambridge: Cambridge University Press, 1983), *passim.* For a discussion of Roman declamation see S. F. Bonner, *Roman Declamation in the Late Republic and Early Empire* (Liverpool: Liverpool University Press, 1969), *passim.*

30. Cicero, *De Oratore* 1. 157.

31. Cicero, *In Verrem* 2. 5. 36.

32. Syme, *The Roman Revolution*, 94.

33. Quintus Cicero, *Commentariolum Petitionis* 2.

34. Cicero, *Brutus* 39.
35. Cicero, *De Oratore* 1. 7.
36. Cicero, *Brutus* 182; *De Oratore* 1. 7.
37. Cicero, *Epistulae ad Familiares* 3. 7. 5.
38. Cicero, *Pro Roscio Amerino* 5. Aulus Gellius, *Noctes Atticae* 15. 28.
39. Cicero, *Pro Roscio Amerino* 8.
40. Cicero, *Pro Roscio Amerino* 6, 127, 131.
41. Cicero, *In Verrem* 1. 49.
42. Cicero, *In Verrem* 1. 45.
43. Cicero, *In Verrem* 1. 47.
44. Cicero, *De Lege Agraria* 2. 8.
45. Cicero, *Paradoxa Stoicorum* 27.
46. Cicero, *Epistulae ad Atticum* 1. 16.
47. Cicero, *Epistulae ad Atticum* 1. 19.
48. Cicero, *Epistulae ad Atticum* 2. 23.
49. Cicero, *Post Reditum in Senatu* 6.
50. Cicero, *Epistulae ad Familiares* 8. 8. 2; *Epistulae ad Quintum Fratrem* 2. 16. 3.
51. Cicero, *Epistulae ad Quintum Fratrem* 2. 16. 1; 3. 6. 4; 2. 15a. 5.
52. Cicero, *Epistulae ad Quintum Fratrem* 2. 15a. 5.
53. Cicero, *Epistulae ad Familiares* 2. 15. 3; 6. 21. 3; 7. 28. 3.
54. Cicero, *De Republica* 3. 3; 1. 48.
55. Cicero, *Pro Marcello* 23.
56. Cicero, *Epistulae ad Atticum* 12. 49.
57. Cicero, *Orationes Philippicae* 6. 2.
58. Cicero, *Epistulae ad Familiares* 7. 1. 4–5. See also *Epistulae ad Familaries* 1. 8. 3–4; 9. 10. 2; 9. 18. 1. *De Officiis* 3. 2.
59. Cicero, *Epistulae ad Familiares* 3. 11. 2; *Pro Balbo* 31.
60. Cicero, *De Officiis* 2. 65–68.
61. Cicero, *De Officiis* 2. 66.
62. Cicero, *De Officiis* 2. 66.
63. Cicero, *De Inventione* 1. 2. *De Natura Deorum* 2. 154.
64. Cicero, *Brutus* 45.
65. Cicero, *Orator* 141. *De Oratore* 1. 14.
66. Cicero, *Partitiones Oratoriae* 130; *De Oratore* 1. 141; *De Inventione* 2. 156.
67. Cicero, *De Officiis* 2. 83; 1. 20; 1. 100; *De Finibus* 5. 65.
68. Cicero, *De Legibus* 1. 21, 23; *Partitiones Oratoriae* 78.

69. Cicero, *De Legibus* 1. 18, 19.
70. Cicero, *De Legibus* 1. 19.
71. Cicero, *De Finibus* 1. 53.

2. The Benefactors of Forensic Discourse

1. For the most recent texts of pre-Ciceronian advocates see *Oratorum Romanorum Fragmenta: Liberae Rei Publica*, ed. Henrica Malcovati, I: Textus (Torino: G. B. Paravia, 1953), *passim*. One Italian study stresses the historical background of the fragments and makes some observations on the style of the individual orators and the influence of Hellenic culture: A. Cima, *L'eloquenza latina prima de Cicerone. Saggio storico-critico* (Rome, 1903), *passim*; cf. *Fifty Years (and Twelve) of Classical Scholarship*, ed. Maurice Platnauer, 2d ed. (Oxford: Basil Blackwell, 1968), 417, 457, n. 4.

2. A. D. Leeman, *Orationis Ratio: The Stylistic Theories and Practice of the Roman Orators, Historians and Philosophers*, vol. 1 (Amsterdam: Adolph M. Hakkert, 1963), 43. S. F. Bonner, "Roman Oratory," in *Fifty Years (and Twelve) of Classical Scholarship*, 2d ed., 417, 420.

3. For a more extended discussion of the need for further research in this period of Roman rhetoric see Richard Leo Enos, "When Rhetoric Was Outlawed in Rome: A Translation and Commentary of Suetonius's Treatise on Early Roman Rhetoricians," *Speech Monographs* [now *Communication Monographs*] 39 (March 1972): 37 *et passim*.

4. The best surveys of this period include M. L. Clarke, *Rhetoric at Rome: A Historical Survey* (London: Cohen and West, 1966), 10–22; J. F. D'Alton, *Roman Literary Theory and Criticism: A Study in Tendencies* (New York: Russell & Russell, 1962), 1–67; J. Wight Duff, *A Literary History of Rome: From the Origins to the Close of the Golden Age*, ed. A. M. Duff, 3d ed. (London: Ernest Benn Limited, 1967), 47–67, 182–94; Bonner, "Roman Oratory," 416–21; George A. Kennedy, *The Art of Rhetoric in the Roman World: 300 B.C.-A.D. 300* (Princeton: Princeton University Press, 1972), 3–102; Leeman, *Orationis Ratio*, vol. 1, 19–66.

5. Cicero, *Epistulae ad Quintum Fratem* 3. 1.

6. In this respect, such a study is also of interest to those who are concerned with the relationship of rhetoric and legal communication in ancient Rome. Surveying contemporary scholarship on Roman oratory, S. F. Bonner has observed that oratory was not an independent study

but so closely conjoined with rhetoric and law that an understanding of the interaction of these disciplines would do much to "aid the progress of knowledge." Bonner, "Roman Oratory," 456–57.

7. J. A. Cook, *Law and Life of Rome* (London: Thames and Hudson, 1967), 8–9.

8. Tacitus, *Dialogus de Oratoribus* 34; Cicero, *Brutus* 305 *et passim*; Plutarch, *Vitae Parallelae: Cicero* 2. 2, 3 *et passim*; Suetonius, *De Rhetoribus* 1; Cicero, *Tusculanae Disputationes* 1. 7.

9. Cicero, *De Amicitia* 1; *Brutus* 307.

10. Cicero, *Brutus* 173.

11. G. L. Hendrickson, *Cicero: Brutus, Orator*, trans. G. L. Hendrickson and H. M. Hubbell (London: Loeb Classical Library, Harvard University Press, 1952), 218.

12. Cicero, *Brutus* 138.

13. Cicero, *Brutus* 143, 207.

14. Cicero, *De Oratore* 1. 95, 213.

15. Cicero, *De Oratore* 1. 77, 106, 164.

16. Cicero, *Paradoxa Stoicorum* 41; *Brutus* 161.

17. Cicero, *Epistulae ad Atticum* 12. 49; *Pro Caecina* 53; *In Verrem* 2. 2. 192.

18. Cicero, *Brutus* 143.

19. Cicero, *Orator* 132.

20. *Oratorum Romanorum Fragmenta*, 237–59.

21. Cicero, *De Oratore* 2. 233.

22. Cicero, *De Oratore* 2. 236; *Brutus* 164–65.

23. Cicero, *De Oratore* 2. 300, 267; *Brutus* 164.

24. Cicero, *Brutus* 143; *De Oratore* 3. 17.

25. Cicero, *Brutus* 143–44.

26. Cicero, *Brutus* 143, 158–59.

27. Cicero, *Brutus* 207, 165; *De Oratore* 1. 82.

28. Cicero, *Orator* 132; *Oratorum Romanorum Fragmenta*, 221–37.

29. Cicero, *Oratorum Romanorum Fragmenta*, 221–37.

30. Cicero, *Brutus* 141–42.

31. Cicero, *Tusculanae Disputationes* 2. 57; *De Oratore* 2. 124, 188.

32. Cicero, *Brutus* 215.

33. Cicero, *Brutus* 139.

34. Cicero, *De Oratore* 3. 13–16.

35. Cicero, *Brutus* 214; *De Oratore* 2. 128–29.

36. Cicero, *De Oratore* 3. 16.

37. Cicero, *Brutus* 215.

38. *Oratorum Romanorum Fragmenta*, 310–30. For further information on Hortensius see Cicero's fragmentary philosophical treatise: M. Tulli Ciceronis, *Hortensius*, edidit commentario instruxit Albertus Grilli (Milano: Instituto Editoriale Cisalpino, 1962).

39. Cicero, *Brutus* 229.

40. Cicero, *Brutus* 320, 323.

41. E. G. Sihler, *Cicero of Arpinum* (New Haven: Yale University Press, 1914), 70. Cf. Cicero, *Divinatio in Caecilium* 24.

42. Cicero, *Hortensius*, "Hortensi Dialogi Forma," 9–11 and especially fragments 33, 35–36, 39.

43. Cicero, *De Oratore* 3. 229–30.

44. Cicero, *Brutus* 301. Cf. *Tusculanae Disputationes* 1. 59; *Divinatio in Caecilium* 39; Quintilian, *Institutio oratoria* 2. 1. 11–12; 10. 6. 4.

45. Cicero, *Brutus* 325.

46. Cicero, *Brutus* 317.

47. Cicero, *Brutus* 303, 325.

48. This phenomenon is so central to the topic that a chapter will be devoted to the composition of image in Cicero's forensic rhetoric.

49. Cicero *De Officiis* 2. 67.

50. Cicero, *Orator* 141.

51. Cicero, *Orator* 143; *De Legibus* 1. 14.

52. Cicero, *De Oratore* 1. 234–43.

53. Cicero, *Orator* 145.

54. Cicero, *Brutus* 212.

55. Richard Leo Enos, "The Epistemological Foundation for Cicero's Litigation Strategies," *Central States Speech Journal* 26 (Fall 1975): 208.

56. Cicero, *Brutus* 145; *Pro Balbo* 45.

57. Cicero, *Divinatio in Caecilium* 57.

58. Cicero, *Brutus* 155; *De Oratore* 1. 180; 2. 24; 2. 140–41; 2. 222.

59. Cicero, *De Oratore* 1. 180. Cf. *Brutus* 145.

60. Cicero, *Brutus* 151. For an example of Cicero's admiration of Servius Sulpicius Rufus see *Epistulae ad Familiares* 4. 3. 1 *et passim*.

61. Cicero, *Brutus* 203–4.

62. Cicero, *Brutus* 145.

63. Cicero, *Brutus* 152.

64. Cicero, *Brutus* 152–54.

65. Cicero, *Brutus* 64. For ancient, secondary accounts of the Elder Cato's rhetoric see Aulus Gellius, *Noctes Atticae* 3. 7. 1 *et passim*; 6. 3. 14–55; 10. 3. 19; and Plutarch, *Vitae Parallelae: Cato Maior, Minor*.

66. Cicero, *De Oratore* 1. 171.

67. Quintilian, *Institutio oratoria* 12. 1. 1.

68. Cicero, *Pro Murena* 58. Cf. *Pro Murena* 56. For an analysis of some speeches by Marcus Cato and others see Donald Murray Ayers, "The Speeches of Cicero's Opponents: Studies in *Pro Roscio Amerino, In Verrem.* and *Pro Murena*" (Ph. D. diss., Princeton University, 1950).

69. Cicero, *Pro Murena* 58.

70. Cicero, *De Legibus* 3. 40; *Pro Murena* 67.

71. Cicero, *De Finibus* 2. 76; *De Officiis* 1. 62; *Pro Balbo* 3.

72. Cicero, *Pro Murena* 61–62.

73. Cicero, *De Finibus* 4. 8–9.

74. Walter J. Ong, *Orality and Literacy: The Technologizing of the Word* (London and New York: Methuen, 1982), 99.

3. The Epistemological Foundation

1. Walter J. Ong, *Orality and Literacy: The Technologizing of the Word* (London and New York: Methuen, 1982), 105. Ong cites his earlier work, *The Presence of the Word: Some Prolegomena for Cultural and Religious History* (New Haven and London: Yale University Press, 1967), for a fuller discussion of this point (see especially 56–57).

2. Torsten Petersson, *Cicero: A Biography* (New York: Biblo and Tannen, 1963), 92.

3. Petersson, 92–93.

4. Suetonius, *De Rhetoribus* 1.

5. Platus, *Curculio* 289–90; Cicero, *De Oratore* 1. 47, 102; 2. 75.

6. Alain Michel, "Rhétorique de Philosophie du Droit," in *Rhétorique et Philosophie chez Cicéron: Essai sur les fondements philosophiques de l'art de persuader* (Paris: Presses Universitaries de France, 1960), 445–536.

7. Cicero, *Orator* 14; *De Oratore* 1. 60; *De Officiis* 1. 4, 6, 11–14; *Pro Archia* 1, 2. *De Finibus* 1. 14–15; 5. 26–27; *Tusculanae Disputationes* 1. 29. Cf. *Brutus* 121, 191.

8. Cicero, *De Finibus* 1. 14–15.

9. Cicero, *De Legibus* 1. 21, 23, 33. Cf. *Partitiones Oratoriae* 78.

10. Cicero, *De Legibus* 1. 18–19, 21, 23; *Partitiones Oratoriae* 78.

11. Cicero, *Orator* 16–18.

12. Cicero, *Orator* 17; *De Oratore* 3. 122.

13. Cicero, *Orator* 51.

14. Cicero, *De Fato* 3.

15. Cicero, *De Oratore* 3. 143; *De Natura Deorum* 3. 8. Cicero's desire was to elevate his own forensic rhetoric by uniting wisdom with eloquence through the aid of philosophy: Cicero, *Tusculanae Disputationes* 1. 7.

16. Cicero, *Brutus* 212.

17. Cicero, *De Officiis* 3. 62.

18. Cicero, *Brutus* 151; *Epistulae ad Familiares* 4. 3. 1 *et passim.*

19. Cicero, *Brutus* 152.

20. Cicero, *Orator* 12.

21. Cicero, *Epistulae ad Atticum* 4. 16; *De Officiis* 1. 63; H. A. K. Hunt, *The Humanism of Cicero* (Carlton: Melbourne University Press, 1954), 207.

22. Cicero, *Tusculanae Disputationes* 1. 24; *De Divinatione* 1. 78; *Orator* 62; *Academica* 2. 74.

23. Cicero, *De Oratore* 3. 60.

24. Cicero, *Academica* 2. 108–11.

25. Cicero, *Academica* 2. 64 *et passim.*

26. Cicero, *Academica* 2. 148.

27. Cicero, *Academica* 2. 105–11.

28. Cicero, *Tusculanae Disputationes* 2. 9; *De Oratore* 3. 79–80; *De Natura Deorum* 2. 1; *De Fato* 4.

29. Cicero, *Orator* 13.

30. Cicero, *Academica* 2. 146.

31. For an analysis of the naturalness and simplicity of Roman justice see A. F. Lefroy, "Rome and Law," *Harvard Law Review* 20 (1906–1907), 606–14.

32. Cicero, *Tusculanae Disputationes* 2. 3. Cf. *Brutus* 186; *De Oratore* 1. 53.

33. Cicero, *De Oratore* 2. 178.

34. Cicero, *De Oratore* 2. 30.

35. Cicero, *Topica* 65–66.

36. Cicero, *Partitiones Oratoriae* 10, 136–37; *De Oratore* 2. 332.

37. Tacitus, *Dialogus de Oratoribus* 19; Cicero, *In Verrem* 1. 1. 4; *Pro Sestio* 36.

38. Cicero, *Tusculanae Disputationes* 2. 5; *Divinatio in Caecilium* 2. 55; *De Inventione* 1. 48.

39. Cicero, *De Finibus* 2. 17.

40. Cicero, *De Finibus* 3. 2, 26; 4. 1, 2, 7–8, 77–80; *De Domo sua* 20–21; *Brutus* 120. Cicero found a laudable exception in Stoic oratory

with Marcus Porcius Cato Uticensis: *Brutus* 118; *Paradoxa Stoicorum* 1, 2.

41. Cicero, *De Finibus* 3. 26; *Academica* 1. 35; *Paradoxa Stoicorum* 6–15.

42. Cicero, *De Officiis* 3. 33.

43. Cicero, *De Legibus* 1. 45. Cf. *De Legibus* 1. 25; *Tusculanae Disputationes* 5. 14.

44. Hunt, 58.

45. Cicero, *Divinatio in Caecilium* 5.

46. Quintilian, *Institutio oratoria* 12. 7. 1.

47. Cicero, *Divinatio in Caecilium* 66–67.

4. The Audiences of Cicero's Rhetoric

1. Norman W. DeWitt, "Litigation in the Forum in Cicero's Time," *Classical Philology*, 21 (July 1926): 218.

2. Asconius, *Introd.* 36; Cicero, *Pro Milone* 67.

3. DeWitt, 218, 220.

4. Frank Frost Abbott, *A History and Description of Roman Political Institutions*, 3d ed. (New York: Biblo and Tannen, 1963), 229.

5. Jerome Carcopino, *Daily Life in Ancient Rome*, ed. Henry T. Rowell, trans. E. O. Lorimer (New Haven: Yale University Press, 1970), 188.

6. Carcopino, 188.

7. Carcopino, 187.

8. Cicero, *Tusculanae Disputationes* 2. 3; *Brutus* 186.

9. Cicero, *De Oratore* 1. 120.

10. Cicero, *Orator* 24; *Pro Roscio Comoedo* 29.

11. Cicero, *Tusculanae Disputationes* 3. 79; *De Oratore* 2. 337. On the command of all styles of rhetoric see: *De Oratore* 1. 223, 234; *Orator* 100; *Partitiones Oratoriae* 15; Quintilian *Institutio oratoria* 12. 10. 12.

12. Cicero, *Brutus* 279.

13. Cicero, *Orator* 236; *De Oratore* 3. 150–51. Cf. *Pro Caelio* 27; *De Oratore* 3. 101.

14. Cicero, *De Amicitia* 96.

15. Cicero, *De Oratore* 2. 159; Tacitus, *Dialogus de Oratoribus* 19.

16. Cicero, *In Verrem* 1. 1. 4; *Pro Sestio* 36.

17. Cicero, *Orationes Philippicae* 1. 22; *Pro Roscio Comoedo* 15; *Pro*

Quinctio 5, 10. In fact, the populace became such an important factor in the courts and Senate that Cicero's brother, Quintus, gave him a treatise on audience analysis entitled *Commentariolum Petitiones.*

18. Cicero, *Epistulae ad Atticum* 1. 14.

19. Cicero, *Orator* 107; *Brutus* 242; *Epistulae ad Quintum Fratrem* 3. 1. 13. Cf. *Orationes Philippicae* 1. 37.

20. Cicero, *Brutus* 192.

21. Cicero, *Pro Sulla* 92.

22. Cicero, *In Verrem* 2. 1. 18–19.

23. Cicero, *Epistulae ad Atticum* 1. 17–18; *Pro Cluentio* 65, 68, 73, 120–22; *Orationes Philippicae* 1. 20, 22; 12. 37; *In Verrem* 2. 1. 17; 5. 177–78; *Pro Roscio Amerino* 11–14; *Pro Caecina* 67–68; *Pro Fonteio* 22–23; *Pro Caelio* 3.

24. Quintilian, *Institutio oratoria* 12. 1. 1.

25. Cicero, *Orator* 24. Cf. *Pro Sexto Roscio Amerino* 29.

26. Quintilian, *Institutio oratoria* 6. 2. 8 *et passim.*

27. *Index Verborum in Ciceronis Rhetorica*, ed. Kenneth Morgan Abbott et al. (Urbana: University of Illinois Press, 1964), 438. See also Cicero, *Orator* 128, where he explains *ethos*, which confirms that he was familiar with the term.

28. Cicero, *De Officiis* 1. 130–32; *Epistulae ad Familiares* 6. 10a. 2; *De Oratore* 2. 198.

29. Cicero, *Epistulae ad Familiares* 6. 1. 3. Clear examples of service to the State by prominent advocates are seen in passages eulogizing Lucius Licinius Crassus and Quintus Hortensius Hortalus, which appear respectively in *De Oratore* 3. 1–12 and *Brutus* 1–10.

30. Cicero, *Epistulae ad Atticum* 14. 17a; *Liborum De Re Publica Incertorum Fragmenta* 5. Cf. *De Officiis* 1. 14; *Tusculanae Disputationes* 1. 112.

31. Cicero, *Epistulae ad Familiares* 4. 14. 1.

32. Cicero, *De Senectute* 61. Cicero did, however, lament the death of Hortensius as the loss of his *auctoritas* and *prudentia.*

33. Cicero, *Paradoxa Stoicorum* 46; *In Verrem* 2. 3. 3; 2. 5. 36; *Pro Caelio* 73.

34. Cicero, *De Officiis* 2. 51; Quintilian, *Institutio oratoria* 12. 7. 1.

35. The concern for manifesting a moral character is mentioned throughout Cicero's forensic orations. Representative passages include *Pro Cluentio* 42; *Pro Murena* 43; *Divinatio in Caecilium* 27; *In Verrem* 2. 5. 188–89.

36. Frank Herwitt Cowles, "Gaius Verres: An Historical Study," *Cornell Studies in Classical Philology* 20 (1917): 29. Cicero, *In Verrem* 1. 56.

37. Cicero, *In Verrem* 1. 6; *Pro Scauro* 26.

38. Cicero, *Pro Rabirio Perduellionis* 6.

39. Cicero, *Pro Rabirio Perduellionis* 18.

40. Cicero, *Pro Rabirio Perduellionis* 20.

41. R. A. Bauman, "The Duumviri in the Roman Criminal Law and in the Horatius Legend," *Historia* (Wiesbaden: Franz Steiner Verlag Gmbh, 1969), 17 and n. 119.

42. Suetonius, *Divus Iulius* 12. Furthermore, as a tribune, the prosecutor Labienus legally limited Cicero's defense speech to one half-hour: Cicero, *Pro Rabirio Perduellionis* 6.

43. Cicero, *Pro Rabirio Perduellionis* 2.

44. Cicero, *Pro Rabirio Perduellionis* 2.

45. Cicero, *Pro Rabirio Perduellionis* 4–5.

46. Cicero, *Pro Rabirio Perduellionis* 5, 6, 9.

47. Cicero, *Pro Rabirio Perduellionis* 19–21.

48. Cicero, *Pro Rabirio Perduellionis* 27.

49. Cicero, *Pro Murena* 11, 3, 7, 54, 56.

50. Cicero, *Pro Murena* 48.

51. Cicero, *Pro Murena* 3.

52. Cicero, *Pro Murena* 24. Cf. 11, 12, 22, and 29.

53. Cicero, *Pro Murena* 25.

54. Cicero, *Pro Murena* 27–28.

55. Cicero, *Pro Murena* 28.

56. Cicero, *Pro Murena* 29.

57. Cicero, *De Oratore* 1. 7.

58. Chaim Perelman and L. Olbrechts-Tyteca, *The New Rhetoric: A Treatise on Argumentation*, trans. John Wilkinson and Purcell Weaver (Notre Dame: University of Notre Dame Press, 1971), 334.

5. The Verrine Orations

1. Donovan J. Ochs, "Rhetorical Detailing in Cicero's Verrine Orations," *Central States Speech Journal* 33 (Spring 1982): 313. In addition to Ochs' essay and the *In Verrem*, the following works provide important information on Cicero, Roman legal procedure, and the trial: E. G. Sihler, *Cicero of Arpinum* (New Haven: Yale University Press, 1914); A. H. J. Greenidge *The Legal Procedure of Cicero's Time* (Oxford: Clar-

endon Press, 1901); Frank Hewitt Cowles, "Gaius Verres; An Historical Study," *Cornell Studies in Classical Philology* 20 (1917); Richard Leo Enos, "Cicero's Forensic Oratory: The Manifestation of Power in the Roman Republic," *Southern Speech Communication Journal* 40 (Summer 1975), 387–88, 393–94.

2. Ochs, 313–14.

3. Cowles, 189–90.

4. Cowles, 190–91. Thomas Stangl, "Pseudoasconiana: Textgestaltung und Sprache," in *Studien zur Geschichte und Kultur des Altertums*, ed. E. Drerup, H. Grimme, and J. P. Kirsch (Paderborn, 1909), 126. Lily Ross Taylor, *Party Politics in the Age of Caesar* (Berkeley and Los Angeles: The University of California Press, 1968), 110.

5. Ochs, 317.

6. Ochs, 318.

7. Ochs, 311. For a general introduction to the concept of heuristics see Susanne K. Langer, *Philosophy in a New Key: A Study in the Symbolism of Reason, Rite, and Art*, 3d ed. (Cambridge: Harvard University Press, 1976), 126.

8. Kritias, *Poetische Fragmente* 88. B2, *Die Fragmente der Vorsokratiker*, ed. Hermann Diels and Walther Kranz, zweiter band (Dublin: Weidmann, 1972); W. B. Stanford, *The Sound of Greek: Studies in the Greek Theory and Practice of Euphony* (Berkeley and Los Angeles: University of California Press, 1967), 1, n. 4; George Kennedy, *The Art of Persuasion in Greece* (Princeton: Princeton University Press, 1963), 4; G. S. Kirk, *Homer and the Epic* (Cambridge: Cambridge University Press, 1965), 1–32; Tony Marion Lentz, "The Oral Tradition of Interpretation: Reading in Hellenic Greece as Described by Ancient Authors" (Ph.D. diss., University of Michigan 1979), especially 278–88; F. David Harvey, "Greeks and Romans Learn to Write," in *Communication Arts in the Ancient World*, ed. Eric A. Havelock and Jackson P. Hershbell (New York: Hastings House, Publishers, 1978), 64.

9. In addition to the references cited in the previous note, see: Richard Leo Enos, "The Hellenic Rhapsode," *Western Journal of Speech Communication* 42 (Spring 1978): 134–43.

10. Jackson P. Hershbell, "The Ancient Telegraph: War and Literacy," *Communication Arts in the Ancient World*, 88, 90. Richard Leo Enos and Jeanne L. McClaran, "Audience and Image in Ciceronian Rome: Creation and Constraints of the *Vir Bonus* Personality," *Central States Speech Journal* 29 (Summer 1978): 98–101. For an interesting discussion

of the subject see: Walter J. Ong, *Orality and Literacy: The Technologizing of the Word* (London: Methuen, 1982), 16–30.

11. Richard Leo Enos, "The Persuasive and Social Force of Logography in Ancient Greece," *Central States Speech Journal* 25 (Spring 1974): 4–10.

12. James J. Murphy, *Rhetoric in the Middle Ages: A History of Rhetorical Theory from St. Augustine to the Renaissance* (Berkeley and Los Angeles: University of California Press, 1974), 9. James J. Murphy, "Rhetoric in Fourteenth-Century Oxford," *Medium AEvum* 34 (1965): 2. L. D. Reynolds and N. G. Wilson, *Scribes and Scholars: A Guide to the Transmission of Greek and Latin Literature* (London: Oxford University Press, 1968), 86. When Cicero was approximately sixty years old, he wrote the *Partitiones Oratoriae* and relaxed the stringent schematic structuring he presented in the *De Inventione Rhetorica*: *Partitiones Oratoriae* 27, cf. 9. Yet prior to the *In Verrem*, no other schematic procedure for structuring argument is put forth by Cicero other than what is offered in *De Inventione Rhetorica*.

13. For a detailed explanation of these concepts see Cicero, *De Inventione Rhetorica* 1. 19–109. Cicero does not initially include *digressio* as one of the components but later lists it as an option: *De Inventione Rhetorica* 1.19, 97. Since *digressio* is acknowledged by Cicero as being either a separate component of an oration or dispersed throughout a speech, it is discussed in this study when appropriate.

14. Cicero, *De Inventione Rhetorica* 1. 19–26.

15. Cicero, *De Inventione Rhetorica* 1. 27–30.

16. Cicero, *De Inventione Rhetorica* 1. 31–33.

17. Cicero, *De Inventione Rhetorica* 1. 33–77.

18. Cicero, *De Inventione Rhetorica* 1. 78–96.

19. Cicero, *De Inventione Rhetorica*, 1. 78.

20. Cicero, *De Inventione Rhetorica* 1. 97.

21. Cicero, *De Inventione Rhetorica* 1. 98–109.

22. In order to avoid unnecessary citation, repetition, and paraphrasing, Cicero's arguments will be selectively cited. References to Cicero's actual phrasing can be found by noting the respective sections analyzed.

23. Cicero, *In Verrem* 1. 18. 55.

24. George A. Kennedy, *Classical Rhetoric and Its Christian and Secular Tradition from Ancient to Modern Times* (Chapel Hill: University of North Carolina Press, 1980), 4–5.

25. Although fragments of forensic arguments are available there is no

artifact which approaches the category of a *Divinatio*: *Oratorvm Romanorvm Fragmenta: Liberae Rei Pvblicae*, ed. Henrica Malcovati, I: Textus (Torino: G. B. Paravia, 1953), *passim.*

26. Cowles, 189–91. Stangl, 126. Taylor, 110.

27. Richard Leo Enos, "The Forensic Oratory of Marcus Tullius Cicero: The Development and Application of a Practical Rhetoric" (Ph.D. diss., Indiana University 1973).

28. Cicero, *Partitiones Oratoriae* 9, 27.

29. Ochs, 317–18.

6. Legal Rhetoric in Theory, Practice, and Publication

1. For discussions of Cicero's oratorical and literary influence see: John C. Rolfe, *Cicero and His Influence* (New York: Cooper Square Publishers, Inc., 1963); and E. K. Rand, *The Aquinas Lecture, 1945: Cicero in the Courtroom of St. Thomas Aquinas* (Milwaukee: Marquette University Press, 1946).

2. Cicero, *De Oratore* 1. 14; Quintilian, *Institutio oratoria* 9. 4. 3–4; Cicero, *Tusculanae Disputationes* 1. 5.

3. Richard Leo Enos, "When Rhetoric Was Outlawed in Rome: A Translation and Commentary of Suetonius's Treatise on Early Roman Rhetoricians," *Speech Monographs* [now *Communication Monographs*] 39 (March 1972): 37.

4. Cicero, *Brutus* 91. 315–16. *The Oxford Classical Dictionary*, ed. N. G. L. Hammond and H. H. Scullard, 2d ed. (Oxford: Clarendon Press, 1970), 234.

5. Cicero, *De Oratore* 1. 47.

6. Cicero, *De Optimo Genere Oratorum* 20–23.

7. Cicero, *De Oratore* 1. 102.

8. Cicero, *De Oratore* 2. 75.

9. Cicero, *De Oratore* 1. 5. Cf. *M. Tulli Ciceronis De Oratore Libri Tres*, comm. Augustus S. Wilkins (Hildesheim: Georg Olms Verlagsbuchhandlung, 1965), 82–83.

10. Cicero, *Orationes Philippicae* 2. 42–43, 84, 101.

11. Cicero, *De Oratore* 1. 203; *Partitiones Oratoriae* 15; *Orator* 123. Cf. *De Oratore* 2. 340–41.

12. Cicero, *De Legibus* 2. 18; *Orator* 221.

13. Cicero, *Orator* 122. Cf. *De Oratore* 2. 99–104.

14. Cicero, *De Oratore* 3. 188.

15. Cicero, *De Oratore* 2. 307–8.

16. Cicero, *Orator* 47–48, 123.

17. For a more detailed explanation of the phrase "quasi-logical," see Perelman and Olbrechts-Tyteca, 193–260, especially 255–60. The terms "illogical" and "extralogical" are used respectively in the conventional sense of errors in rational argument and nonlogical emotive or ethical appeals. The specific meaning of all three terms, however, will be explicated through the analyses of representative orations.

18. Cicero, *Pro Quinctio* 10.

19. Cicero, *Pro Quinctio* 32.

20. Cicero, *Pro Quinctio* 36, 45. Cf. 38, 41, 54.

21. Cicero, *Pro Quinctio* 73.

22. Cicero, *Pro Roscio Amerino* 59; *The Oxford Classical Dictionary*, 236.

23. Cicero, *Pro Roscio Amerino* 13.

24. Cicero, *Pro Roscio Amerino* 17–19, 21.

25. Cicero, *Pro Roscio Amerino* 21.

26. Cicero, *Pro Roscio Amerino* 11, 28, 35.

27. Cicero, *Pro Roscio Amerino* 61; cf. 43, 44, and 58.

28. Cicero, *Pro Roscio Amerino* 50.

29. Cicero, *Pro Roscio Amerino* 88.

30. Cicero, *Pro Caecina* 53–69.

31. Richard Leo Enos, "Cicero's Forensic Oratory: The Manifestation of Power in the Roman Republic," *Southern Speech Communication Journal* 40 (Summer 1975): 394.

32. Cicero, *Pro Roscio Comoedo* 28–30.

33. Cicero, *Pro Roscio Comoedo* 43.

34. Cicero, *Pro Roscio Comoedo* 44.

35. Cicero, *Pro Roscio Comoedo* 17, 20 *et passim.*

36. Cicero, *Pro Roscio Comoedo* 21.

37. Cicero, *Pro Fonteio* 3, 6.

38. Cicero, *Pro Fonteio* 17, 19.

39. Cicero, *Pro Fonteio* 13–15.

40. Cicero, *Pro Fonteio* 12, 23.

41. Cicero, *Pro Fonteio* 21, 22.

42. Quintilian, *Institutio oratoria* 2. 17. 21. Cf. Michael Volpe, "Cicero's 'Dust': Deception, Diversion, or Different Perspective?" *Central States Speech Journal* 29 (Summer 1978): 118–26.

43. Cicero, *Pro Sulla* 88–93. *Pro Flacco* 105–6.

44. Cicero, *Pro Sulla* 89; *Pro Flacco* 106.

45. Cicero, *Pro Rabirio Postumo* 4, 8, 12, 21, 30.

46. Cicero, *Pro Rabirio Postumo* 41–44.

47. Cicero, *Pro Rabirio Postumo* 44.

48. Cicero, *Pro Cluentio* 1, 3, 4, 5.

49. Cicero, *Pro Plancio* 94.

50. For an example of Cicero's attack on forensic argument see *Pro Murena* 25–29.

7. Conclusion: Orality and Literacy

1. Dio Cassius, *Roman History* 40. 53–55. See also Cicero's own remarks in *De Optimo Genera Oratorum* 10.

Bibliography

Primary Sources

The primary sources listed below are standard citations of the Ciceronian corpus. Oxford Classical Texts are often considered to be the most authoritative editions while the Loeb Classical Library series of the Harvard University Press offers the most readable English translations along with the primary text. Cited primary works not available from these two sources are referenced in the bibliography.

1. Letters

Epistulae ad Atticum
Epistulae ad Brutum
Epistulae ad Familiares
Epistulae ad Quintum Fratrem

2. Philosophical Treatises

Academica
De Amicitia
De Divinatione
De Finibus
De Legibus
De Natura Deorum
De Officiis
De Republica
De Senectute
Tusculanae Disputationes

3. Rhetorical Treatises

Brutus or *De Claris Oratoribus*
De Inventione Rhetorica
De Optimo Genera Oratorum
De Oratore
Hortensius (fragmentary)
Orator ad M. Brutum
Partitiones Oratoriae
[Rhetorica ad Herennium]
Topica

4. Speeches

De Domo sua
De Fato
De Haruspicum Responso
De Lege Agraria
Divinatio in Caecilium
De Provinciis Consularibus
In Catilinam
In Pisonem
In Verrem
Oratio in Senatu in togo candida (fragmentary)
Orationes Philippicae
Post reditum ad Populum
Post reditum in Senatu
Pro Archia
Pro Balbo
Pro Caecina
Pro Caelio
Pro Cluentio
Pro Cornelio de maiestate (fragmentary)
Pro rege Deiotaro
Pro Flacco
Pro Fonteio
Pro Lege Manilia or *De Imperio Cn. Pompeii*
Pro Ligario
Pro Marcello
Pro Milone

Pro Murena
Pro Plancio
Pro Quinctio
Pro Rabirio Perduellionis
Pro Rabirio Postumo
Pro Roscio Amerino
Pro Roscio Comoedo
Pro Scauro
Pro Sesitio
Pro Sulla
Oratorum Romanorum Fragmenta. Edidit Henrica Malcovati. I: Textus. Torino: G. B. Paravia, 1953.

5. Poetry

Ciceronis Poetica Fragmenta. Recensuit Antonius Traglia. Roma: Casa Editrice Gismondi, 1950.

6. Reference Works to Primary Sources

Die Fragmente der Vorsokratiker. Ed. Hermann Diels and Walther Kranz. Zweither band. Dublin: Weidmann, 1972.
Documents Illustrating Cicero's Consular Campaign. Trans. Benney R. Reece. Greenville: Furman University Press, 1967.
Hortensius, M. Tulli Ciceronis. Ed. Albertus Grilli. Milano: Instituto Editoriale Cisalpino, 1962.
Index Verborum Ciceronis Epistularum. Ed. Kenneth Morgan Abbott et al. Urbana: University of Illinois Press, 1938.
Index Verborum Ciceronis Poeticorum Fragmentarum. Ed. John William Spaeth, Jr. Urbana: University of Illinois Press, 1964.
Index Verborum in Ciceronis De Inventione. Composuit J. W. Fuchs. Libros II. Gravenhage, Holland: Hage Comitis, 1937.
Index Verborum In Ciceronis Rhetorica. Edited by Kenneth Morgan Abbott et al. Urbana: University of Illinois Press, 1964.
Lexicon zu den Reden des Cicero. Ed. H. Merguet. 4 vols. Jena: Verlag von Hermann Dufft, 1877–1884.
M. Tulli Ciceronis Brutus. Ed. A. E. Douglas. Oxford: Clarendon Press, 1966.
M. Tulli Ciceronis De Oratore Libri Tres. Introduction and notes by Au-

gustus S. Wilkins. Hildesheim: George Olms Verlagsbuchhandlung, 1965.
"Pseudoasconiana: Textgestaltund and Sprache." *Studien zur Geschichte und Kultur des Altertums*. Thomas Stangl. Edited by E. Drerup, H. Grimme, and J.P. Kirsch. Paderborn, 1909.
Roman Civilization: Sourcebook I: The Republic. Edited by Naphtali Lewis and Meyer Reinhold. New York: Harper and Row, 1966.
Studia et Documenta Historia et Iuris. Rome, 1935–.

Ancient Authors and Works

Asconius. *Commentary on Cicero, In Pisonem.*
———. *Commentary on Cicero, In Verrem.*
———. *Commentary on Cicero, Pro Cornelio de maiestate.*
———. *Commentary on Cicero, Pro Milone.*
Aulus Gellius. *Noctes Atticae.*
Cicero (Quintus). *Commentariolum Petitionis.*
Dio Cassius. *Roman History.*
Lex XII Tabularum.
Livy. *Ab Urbe Condita.*
Oratorum Romanorum Reliquiae. Ed. J. Cortese. Turin, 1892.
Platus. *Curculio.*
Plutarch. *Vitae Parallelae: Cicero.*
———. *Vitae Parallelae: Cato Maior, Minor.*
Quintilian. *Institutio oratoria.*
Sallust. *Bellum Catilinae* or *De Catilinae coniuratione.*
———. *Historiae.*
Scriptores Historiae Augustae.
Suetonius. *De Rhetoribus.*
———. *Divus Iulius.*
Tacitus. *Annals.*
———. *Dialogus de Oratoribus.*
———. *Historiae.*
Varro. *De Lingua Latina.*

Secondary Sources

Abbott, Frank Frost. *A History and Description of Roman Political Institutions*. 3d ed. New York: Biblo and Tannen, 1963.

Bibliography

Allen, Walter. "A Survey of Selected Ciceronian Bibliography, 1939–1953." *Classical World* 48 (1953–1954): 129–39.

Ayers, Donald Murray. "Cato's Speech Against Murena." *Classical Journal* 49 (1953–1954): 245–53.

———. "The Speeches of Cicero's Opponents: Studies in *Pro Roscio Amerino, In Verrem,* and *Pro Murena.*" Ph.D. diss., Princeton University, 1950.

Bauman, R. A. "The Duumviri in the Roman Criminal Law and in the Horatius Legend." *Historia.* Wiesbaden: Franz Steiner Verlang Gmbh, 1969.

Bonner, S. F. *Roman Declamation in the Late Republic and Early Empire.* Liverpool: Liverpool University Press, 1969.

———. "Roman Oratory." *Fifty Years (and Twelve) of Classical Scholarship.* Ed. Maurice Platnauer. 2d ed. Oxford: Basil Blackwell, 1968.

Buckley, Michael J. "Philosophic Method in Cicero." *Journal of the History of Philology* 8 (1970): 143–54.

Carcopino, Jerome. *Daily Life in Ancient Rome.* Ed. Henry T. Rowell. Trans. E. O. Lorimer. New Haven: Yale University Press, 1970.

Clark, D. L. *Rhetoric in Greco-Roman Education.* New York: Columbia University Press, 1957.

Clarke, M. L. "Cicero at School." *Greece & Rome* 15 (1968): 18–22.

———. "Ciceronian Oratory." *Greece & Rome* 14 (1945): 72–81.

———. *Rhetoric at Rome: A Historical Survey.* London: Cohen and West, Ltd., 1966.

Cook, J. A. *Law and Life of Rome.* London: Thames and Hudson, 1967.

Costa, Emilo. *Cicerone Giureconsulto.* Edizione Anastatica. Vol. 1. Rome: "L'Erma" de Bretschneider, 1964.

Cowles, Frank Hewitt. "Cicero's Debut as a Prosecutor." *Classical Journal* 24 (1929): 429–48.

———. "Gaius Verres: An Historical Study." *Cornell Studies in Classical Philology* 20. New York: Longman, Green and Co., 1917.

D'Alton, J. F. *Roman Literary Theory and Criticism: A Study in Tendencies.* New York: Russell & Russell, 1962.

Davies, J. D. "Molon's Influence on Cicero." *Classical Quarterly* 18 (1968): 303–14.

DeWitt, N. W. "Litigation in the Forum in Cicero's Time." *Classical Philology* 21 (1926): 218–25.

Donnelly, F. P. *Cicero's Milo: A Rhetorical Commentary.* New York: Fordham University, 1934.

Dorey, T. A. *Cicero*. New York: Basic Books, Inc., 1965.

———. "Cicero, Pompey and the *Pro Archia*." *Orpheus* 2 (1955): 32–35.

Duff, J. Wight. *A Literary History of Rome: From the Origins to the Close of the Golden Age*. Ed. A. M. Duff. London: Ernest Benn Ltd., 1967.

Enos, Richard Leo. "Cicero's Forensic Oratory: The Manifestation of Power in the Roman Republic." *Southern Speech Communication Journal* 40 (Summer 1975): 377–94.

———. "The Epistemological Foundation for Cicero's Litigation Strategies." *Central States Speech Journal* 26 (Summer 1975): 207–14.

———. "The Forensic Oratory of Marcus Tullius Cicero: The Development and Application of a Practical Rhetoric." Ph.D. diss., Indiana University, 1973.

———. "The Hellenic Rhapsode." *Western Journal of Speech Communication* 42 (Spring 1978): 134–43.

———. "The Persuasive and Social Force of Logography in Ancient Greece." *Central States Speech Journal* 25 (Spring 1974): 4–10.

———. "A Rhetorical Analysis of Cicero's Prosecution of Gaius Verres." Master's thesis, Indiana University, 1970.

———. "When Rhetoric Was Outlawed in Rome: A Translation and Commentary of Suetonius's Treatise on Early Roman Rhetoricians." *Speech Monographs* [now *Communication Monographs*] 39 (March 1972): 37–45.

Enos, Richard Leo, and Jeanne L. McClaran. "Audience and Image in Ciceronian Rome: Creation and Constraints of the *Vir Bonus* Personality." *Central States Speech Journal* 29 (Summer 1978): 98–106.

Grant, Michael. *The Roman Forum*. New York: The Macmillan Company, 1970.

Grant, W. L. "Cicero on the Moral Character of the Orator." *Classical Journal* 38 (1943): 472–78.

Greenidge, A. H. J. *The Legal Procedure of Cicero's Time*. Oxford: Clarendon Press, 1901.

Grilli, Albertus, ed. *Hortensius, M. Tulli Ciceronis*. Milano: Instituto Editoriale Cisalpino, 1962.

Grute, Harold. "Cicero's Attitude to the Greeks." *Greece & Rome* 31 (1962): 142–59.

Gwynn, Aubrey. *Roman Education from Cicero to Quintilian*. Oxford: Oxford University Press, 1926.

Hammond, N. G. L., and H. H. Scullard, eds. *Oxford Classical Dictionary*. 2d ed. Oxford: Oxford University Press, 1970.

Harris, Bruce Fairgray. *Cicero as an Academic*. Auckland: University of Auckland, 1961.

Haskell, H. J. *This Was Cicero: Modern Politics in a Roman Toga*. New York: Knopf, 1942.

Havelock, Eric and Jackson P. Hershbell, eds. *Communication Arts in the Ancient World*. New York: Hastings House, Publishers, 1978.

Hendrickson, G. L., and H. H. Hubbell, trans. *Cicero: Brutus, Orator*. Trans. London: Loeb Classical Library, Harvard University Press, 1952.

Hunt, H. A. K. *The Humanism of Cicero*. Carlton: Melbourne University Press, 1954.

Kennedy, George A. *The Art of Persuasion in Greece*. Princeton: Princeton University Press, 1963.

———. *The Art of Rhetoric in the Roman World: 300* B.C.-A.D. *300*. Princeton: Princeton University Press, 1972.

———. *Classical Rhetoric and Its Christian and Secular Tradition from Ancient to Modern Times*. Chapel Hill: The University of North Carolina Press, 1980.

———. "The Rhetoric of Advocacy in Greece and Rome." *American Journal of Philology* 39 (1968): 419–36.

Kennedy, E. J., and W. V. Clausen, eds. *The Cambridge History of Classical Literature. Vol. II: Latin Literature*. Cambridge: Cambridge University Press, 1982.

Kirk, G. S. *Homer and the Epic*. Cambridge: Cambridge University Press, 1965.

Langer, Susanne K. *Philosophy in a New Key: A Study in the Symbolism of Reason, Rite, and Art*. 3d ed. Cambridge: Harvard University Press, 1976.

Leeman, A. D. *Orationis Ratio: The Stylistic Theories and Practice of the Roman Orators, Historians, and Philosophers*. 2 vols. Amsterdam: Adolph M. Hakkert, 1963.

Lefroy, A. F. "Rome and Law." *Harvard Law Review* 20 (1906–1907): 606–14.

Lentz, Tony Marion. "The Oral Tradition of Interpretation: Reading in Hellenic Greece as Described by Ancient Authors." Ph.D. diss., University of Michigan, 1979.

Leon, H. J. "The Technique of Emotional Appeal in Cicero's Judicial Speeches." *Classical World* 29 (1935): 33–37.

Lussky, Ernest Alfred. *The Appeal to the Emotions in the Judicial Speeches of Cicero as Compared with the Theories Set Forth in the De Oratore.* Ph.D. diss., University of Minnesota, 1928.

MacKendrick, P. "Cicero's Ideal Orator." *Classical Journal* 43 (1947–1948): 339–47.

McNally, J. Richard. "Comments on Rhetoric and Oratory in Cicero's Letters." *Southern Speech Communication Journal* 39 (Fall 1973): 21–32.

Marshall, A. J. "Verres and Judicial Corruption." *Classical Quarterly* 17 (1967): 408–13.

Michel, Alain. "L'originalite de l'ideal oratorie de cicéron." *Les Etudes Classiques* 39 (1971): 311–28.

———. *Rhétorique et Philosophie chez Cicéron: Essai sur Les Fondements Philosophiques de L'art de Persuader.* Paris: Presses Universitaires de France, 1960.

Middleton, Conyers. *The Life of M. Tullius Cicero.* Revised edition. London: Gilbert and Rivington, 1837.

Mitchell, Thomas N. *Cicero: The Ascending Years.* New Haven and London: Yale University Press, 1979.

Murphy, James J. *Rhetoric in the Middle Ages: A History of Rhetorical Theory from St. Augustine to the Renaissance.* Berkeley and Los Angeles: University of California Press, 1974.

———. "Rhetoric in Fourteenth-Century Oxford." *Medium Ævum* 34 (1965): 1–20.

Ochs, Donovan J. "Rhetorical Detailing in Cicero's Verrine Orations," *Central States Speech Journal* 33 (Spring 1982): 313–18.

Ong, Walter J. *Interfaces of the Word: Studies in the Evolution of Consciousness and Culture.* Ithaca and London: Cornell University Press, 1977.

———. *Orality and Literacy: The Technologizing of the Word.* London and New York: Methuen, 1982.

———. *The Presence of the Word: Some Prolegomena for Cultural and Religious History.* New York and London: Yale University Press, 1967.

Perelman, Chaim and L. Olbrechts-Tyteca. *The New Rhetoric: A Treatise on Argumentation.* Trans. John Wilkinson and Purcell Weaver. Notre Dame: University of Notre Dame Press, 1971.

Petersson, Torsten. *Cicero: A Biography.* New York: Biblo and Tannen, 1963.

Ramage, Edwin S. "Cicero on Extra-Roman Speech." *Transactions and Proceedings of the American Philological Society* 92 (1961): 481–94.

Rand, E. K. *The Aquinas Lecture: 1945. Cicero in the Courtroom of St. Thomas Aquinas.* Milwaukee: Marquette University Press, 1946.

Reynolds, L. D. and N. G. Wilson. *Scribes and Scholars: A Guide to the Transmission of Greek and Latin Literature.* London: Oxford University Press, 1968.

Rolfe, John. *Cicero and His Influence.* New York: Cooper Square Publishers, 1963.

Russell, D. A. *Greek Declamation.* Cambridge: Cambridge University Press, 1983.

Sattler, William M. "Some Platonic Influences in the Rhetorical Works of Cicero." *Quarterly Journal of Speech* 35 (April 1949): 164–69.

Scullard, H. H. *From the Gracchi to Nero: A History of Rome: 133* B.C.–A.D. 68. London: Methuen, 1963.

Seaman, William, and Carolyn J. Matzke. *Forum Romanum.* Oxford, OH: American Classical League, 1972.

Settle, J. N. "The Trial of Milo and the Other *Pro Milone.*" *Transactions and Proceedings of the American Philological Association* 94 (1963): 268–80.

Sihler, E. G. *Cicero of Arpinum.* New Haven: Yale University Press, 1914.

Shackleton Bailey, David R. *Cicero.* New York: Scribners, 1971.

Solmsen, Frederick. "Aristotle and Cicero on the Orator's Playing Upon Feelings." *Classical Philology* 33 (1938): 390–404.

———. "Cicero's First Speeches: A Rhetorical Analysis." *Transactions and Proceedings of the American Philological Association* 49 (1938): 542–56.

Stanford, W. B. *The Sound of Greek: Studies in the Greek Theory and Practice of Euphony.* Berkeley and Los Angeles: University of California Press, 1967.

Stockton, David. *Cicero: A Political Biography.* London: Oxford University Press, 1971.

Stroux, J. "Summum Ius Summa Inuira." *Romische Rechtswissenschaften und Rhetorick.* Potsdam: Stichnote, 1949.

Sullivan, Francis A. *Cicero's Oratorical Education.* New York: Fordham University Press, 1940.

Syme, Ronald. *The Roman Revolution*. Oxford: Oxford University Press, 1963.

Taylor, Lily Ross. *Party Politics in the Age of Caesar*. Berkeley and Los Angeles: University of California Press, 1968.

Volpe, Michael. "Cicero's 'Dust': Deception, Diversion, or Different Perspective?" *Central States Speech Journal* 29 (Summer 1978): 118–26.

Wilkin, R. N. *Eternal Lawyer: A Legal Biography of Cicero*. London: Macmillan, 1947.

Wilkins, Augustus S., comm. *M. Tulli Ciceronis De Oratore Libri Tres*. Hildesheim: Georg Olms Verlangsbuchhandlung, 1965.

Wooten, Cecil W. *Cicero's* Philippics *and Their Demonsthenic Model: The Rhetoric of Crisis*. Chapel Hill and London: University of North Carolina Press, 1983.

Index

Index

Index

Index

Index

RICHARD LEO ENOS received his Ph.D. in 1973 from Indiana University and performed postdoctoral work at the American School of Classical Studies in Athens in 1974. He has published widely on classical rhetoric and rhetorical theory in journals such as *Rhetoric Society Quarterly*, *Rhetoric Review*, *College Composition and Communication*, and *Communication Monographs*. He has also contributed chapters to *Historical Rhetoric* and *The Present State of Scholarship in Historical and Contemporary Rhetoric* (both edited by Winifred B. Horner) and to *Speech Communication in the Twentieth Century* (edited by Thomas Benson). He currently teaches at Carnegie Mellon University, where he is Associate Professor of Rhetoric and Associate Dean for Academic Affairs, College of Humanities and Social Sciences.